The Food
Combining/Blood Type
Diet Solution

The Food Combining/ Blood Type Diet Solution

A Personalized Diet Plan and Cookbook for Each Blood Type

Dina Khader, M.S., R.D.

with

Irene Toovey

Foreword by John Diamond, M.D.

KEATS PUBLISHING

LOS ANGELES

NTC/Contemporary Publishing Group

The McGraw·Hill Companies

Library of Congress Cataloging-in-Publication Data

Khader, Dina.
    The food combining/blood type diet solution : a personalized diet plan and
    cookbook for each blood type / Dina Khader and Irene Toovey ; foreword by
    John Diamond.
        p.   cm.
    Includes bibliographical references and index.
    ISBN 0-658-00172-8
        1. Blood groups.   2. Nutrition.   3. Weight loss.   4. Health.
    I. Toovey, Irene.   II. Title.

    QP98 .K48   2002
    613.2′5—dc21   00-027511

4 5 6 7 8 9 10 11 12 13   VRS/VRS   2 1 0 9 8 7 6 5 4 3

ISBN 0-658-00172-8

McGraw-Hill books are available at special quantity discounts to use as premiums and
sales promotions, or for use in corporate training programs. For more information, please
write to the Director of Special Sales, Professional Publishing, McGraw-Hill, Two Penn
Plaza, New York, NY 10121-2298. Or contact your local bookstore.

This book is printed on acid-free paper.

For Nigel and Sebastian, who inspired my transformation.

Many people have contributed to the creation of this book: family members, friends, colleagues, and Dina's patients and clients. We are grateful for their support, enthusiasm, and encouragement.

Contents

Foreword

Whatever other modalities may be employed, the cornerstone of every truly therapeutic practice must be sound, individualized nutritional counseling. It is becoming increasingly obvious—even to former skeptics—that every disease has faulty nutrition as one of its causes; and it is frequently the major cause. Thus, every cure must involve nutritional correction. We suffer now from what we have eaten, and will be healed by what we choose to eat instead.

However, for nutritional counseling to be more than merely palliative, patients must be encouraged to adopt the new nutrition not just to help overcome a specific illness but to actively promote positive health: the embracing of health and life. Then there is no regression back to the old ways when the symptoms are relieved.

Every choice for health facilitates the next choice, and then the next, so that one positive nutritional choice leads to many more, all building on each other and enhancing our life energy, the healing power within. And it is this alone that cures.

Thus, effective nutritional counseling must do more than merely offer lucid, correct advice; it must also facilitate positive health choices so as to raise one's innate healing power. It must be inspirational.

For these reasons, I strongly recommend this most helpful book.

—John Diamond, M.D.

Acknowledgments

Many of us are looking for the optimum diet for health and fitness. In my ten years of practice, I have found that working with blood types has not only balanced out weight but also significantly improved a person's total health.

I am very pleased that one of my patients, Irene Toovey, was inspired to help me write one of the few books ever published on this topic. I hope that it will be meaningful to all those searching for optimal health.

I wish to give special thanks to many individuals. These people have professionally changed and shaped my growth and understanding of integrative medicine and nutrition:

- My professors at New York Medical College, especially John Pinto, Ph.D., for his dynamism
- FAIM (Foundation for the Advancement of Innovative Medicine), the medical association responsible for getting alternative medicine accepted in the state of New York
- American Biologics for their well-organized symposiums, bringing together some of the greatest researchers
- Peter D'Adamo, N.D., whose research on blood types truly inspired me
- Khem Shahani, Ph.D., for his work on DDS-1 acidophilus
- John Ionescu, Ph.D., for his passion for research
- Jeff Bland, Ph.D., whose knowledge never ceases to amaze me
- John Diamond, M.D., for his commitment to food combining and the blood type program
- Jeff Moss, D.D.S., for his love of writing on all aspects of nutrition
- National Enzyme for manufacturing the Khader Group formulas

Heartfelt thanks to:

- Gino Cavallo, who strongly encouraged me to hear Peter D'Adamo lecture in 1990 despite my extreme skepticism. This was the turning point in my career.

- Pat Defeo, my personal trainer, who taught me more about life and weight training
- Jennifer Carman, who taught me to listen to my intuition
- Mary Pat Hughes, M.S., R.D., who has always supported my work from day one
- Phyllis Herman, M.Ed., M.S., C.N.S., who edited the manuscript and saw the significance of this book
- Peter Hoffman, my publisher, whose enthusiasm kept me going
- Rani Nasser, whose computer genius formatted the book
- Marvelle Gilbert, my patient and proofreader, whose humor is irresistible
- Norma Bandak and Edith Weichbrodt, two of my best supporters
- Kathy Zill, who runs my office well
- Alison Kallman, M.D., whose cheerfulness will dispel all despairs
- Andrea Hiel, who taught me the European way of nutrition

Finally, each day I thank God for my wonderful parents, whose deep love and encouragement I cannot forget; my sister Randa, who has always believed in me; my youngest sister Nada for her concern about humanity; and Faris, the best brother in the world. I am also so grateful for Friskie and Husky, the most loyal dogs I know.

I am very appreciative of all my patients and anyone who has either directly or indirectly supported my work. Their trust and belief in me will keep me going.

—Dina Khader

Introduction

You are about to embark on a new way of eating that could possibly change your life forever. It certainly changed mine.

Let me begin by telling you about my own miraculous transformation. I was a forty-five-year-old, 170-pound (and expanding by the minute), 5-foot 7-inch gourmet cook with an obsession with eating. My mind was forever focused on what I was going to prepare or eat. I would eat from emotion, choosing meals based on what I craved. I thought I understood good nutrition: a well-balanced meal consisted of a protein, starch, and a vegetable. Well, doesn't it? I always used the freshest and finest ingredients, but despite being a literate and well-educated individual, I knew little about proper eating habits.

For example, I never ate breakfast. Several cups of coffee in the morning did the trick in supplying the energy and vitality that I needed to start the day.

At lunchtime, I was so ravenous that I really could eat everything *including* the kitchen sink. I'd get into my car in a sort of frenzy, salivating about eating an eggplant or chicken Parmesan wedge. Sometimes I would indulge in two to three slices of exotic pizza. I loved to wash this all down with at least one liter of Diet Coke. No wonder my bladder always seemed to hurt and was perpetually distended.

When I came home from work in the late afternoon, I would ransack the kitchen for a pre-dinner snack. I would munch indiscriminately on whatever was available. Of course, I also extensively sampled everything I prepared for dinner.

Dinner was served at around 8 P.M. It was usually deliciously rich and heavy and would zap whatever bit of remaining energy that was left in my body. I would quench my thirst, during and after dinner, with an additional liter of Diet Coke.

You would think that I would have been satisfied by such a gourmet repast, but alas, not I. Ten o'clock or thereabout was a great time to snack on a half a bag of "low-fat" pretzels. Why not? They were low-fat, after all.

These patterns were habitual, and I often promised myself that one day I would seriously try to diet. None of my clothes fit any longer. I was buying larger- and larger-sized outfits to accommodate and hide my expanding physique. My husband would subtly try to suggest that I needed to do something about my mammoth posterior and thunder thighs. I decided to work out on a Thighmaster. Alas, this only created a new problem. I tore the cartilage in one of my knees, which required orthopedic surgery.

In desperation, I mentioned my plight to a colleague who had lost 70 pounds on a diet designed by nutrition consultant Dina Khader, who, I was told, tailors each person's diet to his or her individual needs. Dina's practice was so successful that I had to wait nearly two months to get an appointment to see her.

The Diet and How It Works

I will always think of the day that I met Dina Khader as my day of enlightenment. She explained that losing weight would require significant changes in my dietary habits. Her suggestions would also, soon thereafter, dramatically improve my general health.

She spoke very softly and quickly. I held on to every precious word as though they were pearls of wisdom. Oddly enough, they were enormously helpful and they really made sense. She devised an individualized diet for me that was based on my health issues and blood type, which was A.

Each blood type digests and chemically reacts to foods differently. Proper food selection based on blood type can be a key factor in promoting weight loss, as well as good health.

Dina told me that, as an A blood type, I was best suited to a mostly vegetarian diet, as I had low levels of hydrochloric acid in my system and therefore would have difficulty digesting meat. My new diet was to include vegetables, fruits, nuts, seeds, eggs, lean fish, soy products, and an occasional meal of organic turkey or chicken. I could indulge in an organic beef or lamb meal once a month, although this was not recommended.

Foods containing wheat, such as bread, pastries, pretzels, pasta, and most cereal starches (a major part of my existing diet), were to be eliminated during the dieting period. Adhering to this would be an essential key to losing weight. Dina explained that wheat gluten is a substance that induces allergies, is hard to digest, and can even contribute to depression in some individuals.

I panicked at the thought of giving up my favorite foods. No more scrumptious breads, pasta dishes, and luscious baked goods? Pizza a no-no? How could I stick to such a ridiculous requirement? I despondently looked in the mirror and 170 pounds looked back at me. I had no other choice but to give it a try.

The essence of the diet was based on the concept of food combining. The bad news is that the basic premise of food combining is never to mix a protein and a starch in the same meal (no more steak and potatoes!). The good news is that as long as you combine your foods properly (meat with salad and low-carbohydrate veggies or pasta with salad and any veggie you wish), you can eat as much as you like! This made all the difference to me since I am a big eater and was worried that restricted portions would leave me feeling forever hungry. However, this didn't mean that I had a green light to overeat. Dina told me that I should eat only until I felt comfortably satisfied.

The rationale behind food combining makes a lot of sense. When a starch and a protein are eaten together, it can take the body six hours or longer to digest. Thus, your body must work overtime to break down the foods you have eaten instead of using this metabolic energy to burn off your fatty deposits. On the other hand, it takes less than half the time to digest a perfectly combined meal. A nonstarchy vegetable meal (a big salad) takes about two hours to digest; meals composed simply of fruit can digest in less than forty-five minutes.

Dina recommended a fruit meal as an optimal breakfast choice for me. She told me to eat fruit at least twenty minutes before or thirty minutes after a properly combined meal. I learned that fruits should never be eaten with either protein or starch since that combination would ferment in the stomach. When eaten at the appropriate time, fruits can provide high levels of energy due to the enzymes in them; they will also help to cleanse the digestive system.

Moreover, if the principles of food combining are followed, you will not only lose weight, but you will have more energy.

Other features of Dina's program: milk products were allowed, but in strict moderation. I was permitted to eat fresh mozzarella cheese, organic low-fat yogurt, goat's milk products, organic cow's milk (in small quantities), and moderate amounts of organic sweet butter. Dina told me that goat's milk is often a better choice than cow's milk because it has a similar nutritional profile to mother's milk. Goat's milk and goat's milk products can be less allergenic, less mucous producing, and also less likely to be contaminated with hormones and antibiotics.

According to the blood type theory of nutrition, soy milk and soy products are healthier than cow's milk for the O and A blood types. The mucus-producing effect of soy is nil, and too much mucus in the body is a major allergy, asthma, and yeast inducer. Mucus also prevents the body from building up total immunity. I found that vanilla soy milk was a palatable substitute for cow's milk in my coffee, although this did take a few days to become accustomed to. Yes, I was allowed to have one to two cups of coffee per day! That was the clincher for me. Coffee in moderation was actually considered to be a beneficial beverage for me as an A blood type. Had I been told to give up my coffee, I might not have been able to follow through with this dramatic change of life.

I was encouraged by Dina to use salad dressings, condiments, and seasonings that were free of chemical additives or sugar. I avoided white, balsamic, and red wine vinegars and, instead, used vinegar-free salad dressing. Vinegar can suspend salivary digestion and slow the digestion of starches; it can also increase yeast in the body. Another major problem with vinegar is that it is not well digested and can be a stomach/intestinal irritant that is too acidic on the joints. Raw cold-pressed apple cider or brown rice vinegar is less damaging, but fresh lemon juice is an even better substitute.

The final rule concerned beverages. Herbal teas and water (noncarbonated only) were the best for me. Carbonated waters can cause bloating. I could drink fifteen minutes before a meal or one hour after. Drinking during a meal was a no-no; it can interrupt and slow the digestive process.

Dina also recommended that I add exercise to my daily regime. Exercise would stimulate my metabolism, which would, in turn, speed up the rate of my weight loss.

The quest to attain the proper body weight for my height (approximately 135 to 140 pounds) was on. I left Dina's office with my head spinning with many new ideas. I was overwhelmed. It was as though I was an infant who was learning to walk for the first time. Determined to succeed, I established a workable routine.

I would start off my morning with two cups of coffee with vanilla soy milk. When I arrived at work I would have a fruit breakfast, which usually consisted of either fresh pineapple or a seasonal fruit, such as grapes or berries.

A typical lunch consisted of a mesclun green salad with a variety of leafy sprouts and a protein (poached salmon, tuna, chicken, egg, or turkey). Occasionally, I would have brown rice and sautéed vegetables, or garlic escarole and roasted fennel. A favorite lunch was spinach and mushroom salad topped with fresh feta cheese and a lemon-oregano-garlic dressing.

I always followed the drinking rules and quenched my thirst at the appropriate times with a variety of herbal teas.

When I returned home from work, I would have a snack of organic carrot juice, fruit, or an organic yogurt—plain, vanilla, or cappuccino. Sometimes I would grab a handful of nuts or seeds, which provided that extra burst of energy that I needed to prepare dinner.

Dinner protein was usually turkey, fish, or organic chicken. Lamb or beef was limited to once a month; chicken was allowed up to three times a week. A salad and vegetables always accompanied the protein. The portions could be as large as I desired, so I always felt extremely satisfied. After a while, I found myself wanting smaller amounts of protein and started eating more salad and vegetables. An hour after dinner, I would enjoy a flavorful cup of herbal tea. If I needed a snack, a rare occurrence, I would eat a piece of fruit thirty or more minutes after dinner.

Dining out was simple. Every restaurant accommodated my dietary needs. Even my vacation on an obscure Caribbean island posed little difficulty. Here's more good news! I was permitted to have one to two glasses of wine before my meal. A good dry wine is especially compatible with a protein meal, and it helps the digestive process. I also sometimes indulged in a cappuccino after dinner.

When I dine out, I always order a plain dish of grilled fish or chicken (without sauces or gravies) plus a vegetable. I start my meal with a mixed green salad. All you really need to do is replace the rice or potato that is usually included with a restaurant meal for a salad or vegetable. Some Chinese restaurants offer steamed fish, tofu, or vegetables with delicious dipping sauces that are cornstarch- and sugar-free. (Be aware, however, that most soy sauces contain wheat gluten.)

My Success Story

How much did I lose? I was 40-plus pounds lighter after eight months. Dina then put me on a maintenance diet that included whole grain breads, cereals, oatmeal, and pasta on a twice-a-week basis. I also added spelt products to my diet. I found many tasty products made from this healthful wheat substitute.

To be honest, I am quite content to remain on the original diet forever. Once again I have a sexy figure that resembles the one that I had twenty years ago. My husband has a renewed attraction and interest in me. Friends keep on staring at me with wonder. They claim that I look years younger. I have much more energy, and my creativity was at an all-time high while I helped create this book.

Unfortunately, as far as my checkbook is concerned, my entire closet had to be cleared to make way for a new wardrobe. I went from a size 16 to less than an 8 in most items. When I tried on my clothes to figure out what could be salvaged, it was incredible to see how my old clothes swam on my new slender figure.

Eighteen months after I began my weight-loss quest, I have maintained the 45-pound weight loss. I never eat wheat products, I still avoid dairy, and I continue to practice food combining. My health has also taken a profound turn for the better.

I suffered from severe allergies since the age of ten. During the spring and fall, I was very often bedridden and incapacitated. By age forty, I developed asthma that required the use of numerous inhalers and occasional shots of adrenaline. I also suffered from chronic bladder infections that caused me great discomfort. My skin was covered with adult acne, and the dermatologist told me I would have to take low doses of antibiotics for an extended period to keep it under control.

All of my conditions are healed as a result of my new dietary habits. The only supplement that I take is a daily probiotic to keep the acne and bladder problems at bay. A probiotic is an acidophilus supplement that provides good bacteria, which helps prevent skin problems and infections. If you would have told me two years ago that a change of eating regime would have health benefits, I would have been very skeptical. These additional dividends are absolutely miraculous to me. That is why I will never go back to my former life of indiscriminate indulgence.

So there you have it—an amazing success story about an ordinary person. You may have related to aspects of it, and perhaps it has inspired you. If so, I would strongly suggest that you consult a physician or a nutritional expert before embarking on this program. Then take the plunge and look forward to a slimmer and healthier body.

Read on as Dina takes over and explains the nuts and bolts of her program.

—Irene Toovey

CHAPTER ONE

Principles of the Program

True health is a combination of many factors. It involves good nutrition, fresh unpolluted air, moderate exercise, adequate sunshine, rest, good hygiene, and an optimistic outlook on life.

In my practice, I focus on good nutrition as it relates to building health, utilizing both the blood type theory and food combining principles. I also recommend nutritional supplements, which help significantly in both weight reduction and health improvement. In my ten years of practice, the results in weight loss for my clients have been dramatic.

Food Combining

The concept of food combining was introduced over sixty years ago by Dr. William Howard Hay, a talented surgeon and general practitioner. He suggested that incorrect chemical conditions are the underlying cause of disease and that compatible food combinations are nature's way of reestablishing and maintaining the body's proper chemical balance. When one consumes too many different types of food at one time, internal poisoning can result, depressing energy levels, adding weight, and even initiating disease.[1]

Protein foods such as meat, fish, poultry, and eggs must be broken down and absorbed by the body in an acid environment aided by pepsin, an enzyme that exists only in an acid medium. If foods that require an alkaline enzyme (i.e., starches and carbohydrates) are eaten with a protein meal, then digestion can be seriously compromised. What results is a chemical reaction between the acid enzyme and the alkaline enzyme, causing a neutralization reaction rendering both enzymes ineffective.[2] Digestion stops, and food sits in the intestinal tract for hours. The result: gas and bloating.

ACID + BASE = NEUTRAL SOLUTION

In this neutralized environment, the protein in the meal does not get properly metabolized, and, as a result, it is absorbed intact as large protein molecules that contain histamines (a toxic protein), which can lead to allergies like asthma, eczema, hay fever, and migraines. Starches or carbohydrates, on the other hand, require an alkaline environment for digestion and absorption. The starch is initially broken down in the mouth by the enzyme ptyalin and then transported into the small intestine, where it is eventually absorbed by the body.

The Allergy Connection

Many of my patients with hidden food sensitivities have improved significantly simply by following proper food combining. The key to losing weight, beyond counting calories and fat, is how well one's digestion works. More efficient digestion will result in faster metabolism of food and, ultimately, weight loss. Food allergies should not be confused with food sensitivities or intolerances. A food allergy triggers an immune response provoking an antibody effect. On the other hand, food sensitivities or intolerances disrupt digestive functions.

Sometimes specific foods are the culprit in weight gain. After eliminating an allergy-inducing food, excess pounds may drop away. Often one tends to overeat these allergenic foods, creating toxicity. The body's response is to dilute the toxin by transporting fluid to the area, causing swelling or edema. Edema is simply excess fluid retention, which can occur anywhere in the body. Overweight and obese people all carry excess water

Symptoms Produced by Poor Food Combinations

Environmental allergies

Gas

Bloating

Constipation

Indigestion

Inflammation

Weight gain

Migraines

Sluggishness

weight. Thus, when a considerable amount of weight is lost in the first two weeks of almost any diet, most of the initial weight loss is water. Foods that become toxic also affect the appestat, the appetite control center in the brain, rendering it insensitive to feelings of satiety. Thus, one's appetite can rage out of control.

Finally, when toxins reach the intestines, they damage digestive enzymes interfering with food metabolism. Poorly digested food is then stored as body fat.

Food allergies can affect every organ system, and symptoms can vary across the board—from irritability and other negative moods to life-threatening conditions such as anaphylactic shock. Physical symptoms, such as puffiness under the eyes, fatigue, runny nose, intestinal disturbances, headaches, insomnia, and fluid retention, all signal food sensitivities. It is more common to be sensitive to several foods rather than just one. Wheat, dairy, corn, citrus (including tomatoes), peanuts, soy, yeast, and sugar are foods that most commonly produce fluid retention. These are also the foods that can cause and aggravate an existing inflammatory condition, such as arthritis or asthma.[3]

In my experience, the blood type approach has been very accurate in determining possible food allergies and sensitivities. Occasionally, I do come across clients who react to foods that are normally beneficial to their blood type.

Other Issues

A major dietary faux pas that many of us make is to eat fruits together with other foods. This often leads to intestinal gas, bloating, sluggishness, and slower digestion. Fruits should only be eaten either fifteen minutes before meals or thirty minutes or more after meals for enhanced energy and a happier digestive tract. Fruits can be eaten as snacks as long as they are eaten alone.

Besides bloating, gas, and sluggishness, many types of headaches can be attributed to poor food combinations, which can also sometimes trigger hypoglycemia or hyperglycemia (low or high blood-sugar levels, respectively).

Another habit that can contribute to weight gain is eating too quickly. People have different speeds of eating. The slower the eater, the less likely a weight problem will exist. Many nutritional deficiencies could be eliminated if food were not so quickly gulped down.

The environment in which we eat is also crucial. The pattern of our thoughts can either positively or negatively affect our digestion. A peaceful and happy atmosphere will enhance our digestion, while a noisy or angry environment will significantly interfere with digestion.

With respect to drinking with meals, there are important considerations. A meal that has a naturally high water content (e.g., fresh fruit salad or a raw green salad) can be accompanied by water as a beverage. Since raw fruits and vegetables do not require hydrochloric acid to be broken down, it does not matter that drinking water dilutes the stomach acid. However, when we drink large quantities of water, juice, or sodas with a protein meal (either animal- or vegetable-based), serious consequences can occur. The hydrochloric acid in the stomach is diluted and will either slow transit time in the stomach or negatively affect the efficiency of digestion.

As with everything in life, there are exceptions to the food combining rules. I would not recommend food combining to those who are very underweight. Also, athletes who burn their calories rapidly would lose too much weight being strict food combiners. Those who go for long periods of time without eating (six or more hours) could experience hypoglycemia and may need to combine a little starch with their protein. The best advice I can offer is to listen to the messages of your own body.

It is not uncommon for some people to feel worse before they feel better as they start improving their diet. A withdrawal effect is often experienced, similar to giving up coffee or alcohol. As toxins stored in fatty tissue and organs dump out into the bloodstream, a healing crisis can occur. This process normally clears up within a few days.

The Blood Type Theory

Food Lectins

Lectins are ubiquitous tiny proteins in foods, which selectively cause clumping of red blood cells, white blood cells, and cells of the gastrointestinal tract. If a lectin is compatible with an individual's blood type, better health, immunity, and proper body weight are achieved. When a lectin is incompatible with one's blood type, inflammation occurs and, over time, may lead to food allergies or sensitivities and ultimately, in some cases, degenerative diseases. Some cancer researchers have explored the role that food lectins play in that disease.[4]

Harmful lectins can attack organ systems such as the brain, liver, kidneys, or digestive tract. This creates a clumping of blood cells, which eventually damages the body part. In leukemia, certain lectins can attach themselves to the cell receptors of white blood cells, triggering rapid cell division. This severely elevates the white blood cell count, initiating leukemia. Lectins can either decrease white blood counts or elevate them, depending on the type of lectin. Lectins cause different reactions in different people. One person might develop liver cancer, whereas another might get arthritis. Wherever lectins build up frequently, that part of the body will suffer.[5] Destructive lectins also prevent weight loss by slowing down metabolism and digestion or inhibiting insulin secretion from the pancreas.

The Evolution of Blood Types

There are four blood types: O, A, B, and AB. Different blood types evolved in different parts of the world at different eras of human history, depending on the environment, susceptibility to disease, and the availability of food.

- *The O blood type* was the first blood type to evolve from the hunter-gatherer era around 50,000 B.C. Since the diet at the time was high in red meat, the group O individuals needed higher amounts of stomach acid in order to digest this animal protein. Even today, when looking at the digestive tract of an O individual, one will see higher amounts of hydrochloric acid in the stomach. The red meat acts as a sponge absorbing the acid. This is why more digestive problems (such as ulcers) may occur in O type individuals who follow a vegetarian diet without animal protein. From a weight standpoint, many blood type O individuals will gain a significant amount of weight following a high-carbohydrate diet, as their bodies cannot properly metabolize these foods. The carbohydrate that has the worst weight-gaining effect for blood type O is the gluten in wheat, which inhibits insulin metabolism and disrupts the efficient burning of calories.[6]

- *The A blood type* formed when man began to develop an agricultural lifestyle between 25,000 and 15,000 B.C. This drastic change from a high-animal protein diet to a more grain- and vegetable-based diet reduced the hydrochloric acid secretion in the stomach. The blood type A individual could no longer break down or metabolize animal protein efficiently. For this reason, the blood type A person does best on a vegetarian diet, emphasizing vegetable proteins such as legumes and nuts. Fish and some poultry products can be included in the diet occasionally. For weight loss, the healthiest diet is a vegetarian diet for blood type A. Meat will be stored as fat in type As. Dairy products are also poorly digested and can inhibit metabolism and/or lead to serious allergies, including environmental allergies or inflammation somewhere in the body.

- *The B blood type* evolved as a balance between the two blood types A and O. The B individual came much later as man traveled further like nomads, searching and exploring new territories. Type B also evolved from the intermingling of blood type O with blood type A. This occurred between 15,000 and 10,000 B.C. The B blood type does very well with raw milk products, such as unpasteurized cheeses and yogurt, and fairly well with organic low-fat milk. They can also eat a combination diet of both animal protein and vegetable protein. Since B blood types can metabolize dairy products and most foods, they will usually lose weight effortlessly as long as peanuts, corn, wheat, and lentils are eliminated from the diet.

- *The AB blood type* is the most recent to evolve (within the last millennium and a half). This blood group is a combination of groups A and B. For weight loss and maintaining a healthy weight, AB types do best on seafood, dairy, nuts, and grains. Again, wheat products in the form of bread, pasta, or pastries should be avoided for weight loss. In fact, wheat, no matter what a person's blood type, will slow down metabolism and inhibit insulin efficiency. The scientific research supporting this effect has been documented.[7] There are many alternatives to white and whole wheat bread. Rice, oat, or spelt flour makes tasty breads, pasta, cakes, and cookies.

Working with the blood type diets over the years, I have seen remarkable health improvement and weight-loss results. Underweight individuals have also responded well (putting on the required extra pounds) using the blood type approach. The blood type theory has taken the guesswork out of determining which diet is best for which patient. Should he or she follow a vegetarian diet or a meat-eating diet? Do calories count? How much exercise is required? These and many more questions have been largely answered through my experience with the blood type approach.

Blood Type Success Stories

Many of my patients who have had allergies, asthma, and fatigue have reversed their ailments by eating according to the guidelines for their blood types. Patients taking medications for hypothyroidism have been able to either reduce or completely eliminate their medications. Similar results have been seen in patients with hypertension and high cholesterol. Patients who were frequently sick with colds, flus, and other viral infections have boosted their immune systems. Chronic coughs have also completely cleared up. Reflux problems including the latest precancerous form—gastroesophageal reflux disorder (GERD)—have subsided.

Ninety-eight percent of my cancer patients do not lose their hair when they see me at least two weeks prior to chemotherapy. This is due to a combination of both the blood type approach and the probiotic I developed called Intestinal Balance (see Appendix: Preferred Products List). Also, my cancer patients remain strong and healthy when undergoing conventional cancer treatment. Better tolerance to chemotherapy and recovery from chemotherapy are common in my patients. Kidney and liver diseases have also responded well to the blood type diet when it is strictly followed.

My pediatric patients with learning disabilities, such as ADD and ADHD, have experienced positive and dramatic cognitive and behavioral changes. These children are better able to focus and learn in school, and they have less hyperactive behavior.

Patients with autoimmune diseases such as lupus, multiple sclerosis, and other muscle diseases have experienced greater energy and a lessening of their symptoms.

I could go on and on; however, the focus of this book is weight loss.

Exercise

In any serious weight-loss program, exercise is a crucial component. Without exercise, we experience more stress, age faster, are prone to chronic illness, and lose good body and skin tone. With the bloodtyping approach, there are specific exercise prescriptions. The more animal protein in the diet, the more exercise an individual should engage in to burn additional calories. Blood type Os require more exercise (both aerobic and anaerobic) than any other blood type. Most of our greatest athletes have been blood type O. In general, O blood types are less prone to muscle and bone injuries as long as the diet is balanced and nutritional supplements are taken. Blood type As do better with more gentle exercises such as yoga, tai chi, or stretching. However, some aerobic exercises, such as brisk walking or cycling, should be incorporated when trying to lose weight. Blood type Bs and ABs also do well with moderate exercise. The amount and type of exercise will vary depending on the level of fitness and health of the individual. I always recommend both aerobic exercise and weight training for a balanced fitness program. Proper stretching and yoga should also be included to maintain fluidity and flexibility in the muscles and joints. I often also recommend other forms of bodywork, such as the Alexander technique, to improve posture and breathing.

Enzymes for Weight Loss

I believe nutritional supplements are an essential part of a healthy lifestyle. However, the healthier the diet, the fewer supplements are required. The safest supplements I use to enhance weight loss are digestive enzymes. Beyond helping with digestive problems, a well-rounded digestive enzyme formula can help with weight loss. Lipase, the enzyme that assists the body in breaking down dietary and body fat, is especially important.

Studies carried out by Dr. David Galton from Tufts University School of Medicine have shown that obese individuals are deficient in lipase.[8] This enzyme was deficient in both fatty tissue and fatty tumors (lipomas). If deficient in lipase, the body will be more likely to deposit plaque in the arteries and encourage fat buildup in the organs.

Lipase is found only in raw foods. Cooking at 118°F or higher destroys lipase and all other enzymes. The more processed a food, the fewer enzymes it retains, and the easier it will be to gain weight from that food. Calorie for calorie, raw foods are not comparable to cooked foods. It is very difficult to gain weight on a raw-food diet. On the other hand, the pancreas and the pituitary glands can become exhausted through overexertion when cooked foods alone are eaten.

When these glands are overtaxed, sluggishness sets in and the thyroid gland shuts down, resulting in weight gain. Children who overeat have triple the amount of fat cells compared to children who undereat. When both types of children consume the identical amount of calories, the child with more fat cells will gain weight more quickly.

Instilling good eating habits in young children will prevent obesity later on in life. Plenty of raw vegetables and fresh fruits plus enzyme supplements can promise long-term weight-loss results for obese children.

The body's production of enzymes diminishes significantly with age. This is one of the many reasons why it is harder to lose weight as one gets older. Many serious diseases have been tied to enzyme deficiencies. These range from cancer, diabetes, heart disease, high blood pressure, lupus, and multiple sclerosis. Early skin aging can also be traced to enzyme deficiencies.

At one time it was believed that enzymes could not be taken orally, as they would be destroyed by the hydrochloric acid in the stomach. However, research measuring blood levels of individuals taking enzyme supplements has shown that oral enzymes are, in fact, absorbed.[9]

Benefits of Taking Plant Enzymes*

Better absorption of vitamins and minerals

Helps break down fat for weight loss

Improves blood sugar imbalances

Digests cholesterol and triglycerides in the blood

Improves digestion

Eliminates gas and bloating

Slows down aging, including skin aging

Builds and repairs damaged tissues

Reduces inflammation anywhere in the body

Destroys viruses and bacteria

Reduces lactic acid buildup in muscles from overexertion

Can help neurological disorders, including schizophrenia, depression, and obsessive-compulsive behavior

Reduces urinary tract infections

Detoxifies the body

Stimulates the immune system

Slows down graying hair

Improves blood circulation

Reduces water retention

* People with ulcers should consult their health-care practitioner before taking enzyme supplements.

There has also been controversy among practitioners and researchers as to whether the body will become dependent on enzymes if taken long term. Some researchers have hypothesized that whatever enzymes are not used up orally will be stored by the body to build up the enzyme reservoir.[10]

Discussions with enzyme experts have led me to believe that plant enzymes will not shut down the body's own production of enzymes, whereas pancreatic or animal-based enzymes may encourage the body's dependency on pancreatic enzymes. One significant benefit in taking enzymes regularly is that it enhances the absorption of vitamins and minerals from food. Enzymes also provide more energy and a sense of well-being, plus many more benefits as listed in the preceding chart.

Where to Start

When following a new program, it is important to remember that motivation will vary. It is almost impossible to follow everything 100 percent of the time. Socializing, travel, and availability of foods are significant factors. Don't be discouraged; behavior sometimes takes three months to change permanently. Motivation may wane, and working with a nutritionist or health practitioner can make a real difference for some people. This may also be true as far as exercise is concerned. Personally speaking, I have had greater results working out with a trainer rather than on my own. Most of us work harder when someone else is watching.

For openers, I suggest that you eliminate wheat and corn from your diet first, followed by white sugar, artificial sweeteners, and sodas. Research indicates that wheat has a worse effect on insulin levels than fresh fruit or fructose.[11] Corn and corn products are second to wheat.

Why Is Wheat So Bad?

Wheat, like sugar, prevents weight loss. Whole wheat and white flour both inhibit insulin from working properly at removing excess sugar from the blood. Because insulin cannot function optimally, the wheat calories are stored as fat. Wheat tends to be less harmful in A blood types; however, those wishing to lose weight are strongly advised to avoid wheat altogether.

Another problem with wheat is that most of the flour in the United States is bleached, which destroys beneficial nutrients, making the bread or pasta more acidic. Most diseases begin when the body's pH in blood, urine, and saliva becomes acidic.

Here is a list of some products that contain wheat, but be sure to read all food-product labels carefully.

- White/whole wheat bread
- Specialty breads
- Bagels
- Rolls
- Muffins
- Pasta
- Pizza dough
- Pita bread
- Donuts
- Cookies
- Cake
- Pastry
- Thickeners
- Prepared gravy mixes
- Pancakes/pancake mixes
- Waffles
- Chinese noodles (except rice noodles)
- Croutons
- Croissants
- Cereals
- Seasonings
- Frozen doughs
- Pie crust
- Tortilla chips (some flavors)
- Hot dog/hamburger buns
- Biscuits
- Toaster Strudel
- Pop Tarts
- Cream of Wheat, Wheatena
- Bulgur, couscous

The Problem with Sugar

Sugar consumption in the United States is up 30 percent since 1983. The average American consumes over 150 pounds of sugar each year in the form of sucrose, dextrose, glucose, and high-fructose corn syrup. That's more than 20 teaspoons of added sugar a day.[12] Most of the sugar in the American diet comes from soft drinks. Other significant sources are table sugar, processed foods, and baked goods. Children consume two and a half to three times more sugar than adults. That extra sugar adds up over the long term, causing malnutrition, obesity, and an increased susceptibility to cancer and diabetes in later life. A major food allergen, sugar suppresses the immune response and is devoid of enzymes.

Too much sugar encourages insulin secretion from the pancreas. Insulin removes excess sugar from the blood and transports it into muscles for energy, and the excess is stored as fat. Consistently high insulin levels can increase cholesterol production, which can cause heart disease and diabetes over time. Cancer has also been correlated with high insulin levels because the eicosanoids manufactured during elevated insulin levels stimulate immune suppression and promote cancer cell proliferation.[13] Sugar is a tumor feeder.

Sucanat, the first extraction from sugarcane juice, can be used as a refined sugar substitute. Fructose, fruit sugar that resembles white sugar, is considerably sweeter than table sugar. Make sure the fructose is from fruit and not corn. It is more slowly metabolized than regular sugar and therefore more suitable for individuals with blood-sugar problems.

Try Stevia Instead

While I discourage the use of artificial sweeteners, I do recommend a sweet herb called *stevia,* a shrub native to Brazil and Paraguay. Stevia extract can be anywhere from 100 to 300 times sweeter than white sugar.[14] Stevioside, a combination of glucose, sophorose, and steviol, is the major complex molecule responsible for the sweetening power of this small plant.

Stevia does not affect blood-sugar metabolism. Some studies have shown that stevia reduces plasma glucose levels in healthy individuals. Diabetics can use this natural sweetener without any side effects. Stevia may also reduce the growth of plaque on teeth, thus preventing cavities.

Stevia is effective in mouthwashes and toothpastes for oral health. Because stevia does not break down when heated, it is an excellent sweetener to use in baking and cooking. See pages 125 and 128 for dessert recipes that include stevia.

Stevia can be purchased as a powder, as a liquid, or in individual packets. It is available in health-food stores.

Japanese Green Tea as a Weight-Loss Aid

As part of my nutritional weight-loss program, I do recommend drinking two cups a day of Japanese green tea, also called Sencha tea (*Camellia sinensis*). Currently, we do not have sufficient research on other types of green tea, such as Chinese or Indian green tea. Research has shown that drinking green tea twice a day can reduce the growth of excess fat cells. I recommend drinking green tea twenty to thirty minutes before meals to stave off hunger pangs and to suppress the appetite. Green tea can also be drunk between meals.

If you are not a tea drinker and are unwilling to become one, take green tea capsules. Make sure you purchase either the liquid extract form or the soluble powdered form. The higher the percentage of

Benefits of Drinking Japanese Green Tea

Assists in weight loss by reducing the growth of fat cells

Can help regulate blood pressure

Enhances the immune system by helping T-cells and natural killer cells

Encourages bowel regularity

Has a mild stimulating effect

Reduces bacteria in the mouth, preventing bad breath and cavities

Lowers cholesterol by breaking down fat

Destroys viruses, including virulent ones such as herpes, HIV, and polio

Prevents significant free radical damage to healthy tissues

Prevents platelet aggregation, reducing the risk of stroke

Prohibits normal cells from mutating or becoming cancerous

Keeps existing tumors from growing and spreading

polyphenols in the green tea, the more effective it is as both a weight-loss and a healthy aging beverage.

Green tea does contain a small amount of caffeine, depending on the length of time the tea is brewed. If you are caffeine-sensitive, brew for just three minutes. Recent research indicates that there is more benefit to caffeinated green tea as opposed to the caffeine-free or decaffeinated versions. One cup of coffee (automatic drip) has as much caffeine as seven or eight cups of regular green tea. In preparing green tea, use warm water rather than boiling water to fully preserve the antioxidants present in the tea. The antioxidants in green tea are believed to be more effective than taking vitamins C and E.

Green tea is also very helpful in both cancer prevention and cancer treatment. The American Institute for Cancer Research has supported these studies. Drinking ten Japanese-size tea cups daily can significantly shrink tumors of any kind.[15]

Fasting

Proper fasting will improve energy, health, and immunity, and ensure a more efficient metabolism. Thus, I occasionally recommend either a fresh fruit or a fresh vegetable juice fast for one day for healthy individuals. Juice fasting once a week is an effective way to break through a weight plateau; it shocks the metabolism into picking up momentum.

However, those with severe hypoglycemia should not fast unless professionally supervised.

Here is a sample one-day juice fast:

Breakfast: Pineapple Pizzazz

Freshly juiced pineapple (not canned pineapple)

Mid-Morning Energy Pep-Up

Crush watermelon in the blender, or freshly juice in the juicer.

Lunch: Ginger Jazz

Juice:
1 large carrot
2 celery stalks
2 broccoli stalks
1 Kirby cucumber

Mid-Afternoon Cranberry Delight

Juice:
2 Granny Smith apples
1 medium beet
Small piece of ginger ($1/4$ inch)

Dinner: Metabolic Booster

Juice:
1 large carrot
$1/2$ bunch parsley
1 Kirby cucumber
2 broccoli stalks

For those with hypoglycemia, a one-day protein fast will work well. One product that I have had very good results with is Ultra-Clear Plus, a rice-based detoxifying powder that also works very well for weight loss. I have also used Ultra-GlycemX, a soy-based product, with similar results. I usually recommend up to five shakes a day blended with water and crushed ice. The shakes are spaced out every three hours to prevent a hypoglycemic attack. There is also a detoxifying protocol with Ultra-Clear Plus for those wishing to clean out their bodies from environmental toxicity as well as from chemotherapy.

CHAPTER TWO

Success
Stories

In my ten years of clinical practice, I have encountered many different illnesses that have responded well to the blood type program. I have also seen remarkable results with patients who have been able to maintain weight loss for seven or more years.

I would like to share with you a few real-life stories that have had what might be considered "miraculous" results. All of the following patients adhered to the food combining principles outlined earlier.

Sonia's Story

Blood type A, female, 42

Sonia initially met with me for weight loss. She was also experiencing a fertility problem and could not conceive. Another indication of a hormonal imbalance were two ovarian cysts.

Sonia had a very poor diet that was extremely high in red meat and sugar. I recommended a blood type A vegetarian diet and designed a meal plan and supplements program for her. To resolve Sonia's ovarian cysts, I recommended wild yam root and dong quai with royal jelly for progesterone balancing, vitamin E for cysts, and a probiotic (acidophilus and bifidus) supplement. The probiotic was intended to clear up any infection that might be present in the uterus and ovaries. Acidophili is a natural antibiotic that is produced by the DDS-1 strain *Lactobacillus acidophilus.* Magnesium citrate and flaxseed oil (in liquid form) were also recommended to help prevent further cyst formations and to reduce the cyst size. To enhance Sonia's weight loss and nutrient absorption of vitamins and minerals from food, I suggested an enzyme formula called Enzymes 2000, a product that I developed for my patients (see Appendix: Preferred Products List).

Throughout her visits with me, her physician, a specialist in infertility, monitored Sonia. Within six weeks, Sonia lost 10 1/2 pounds, which delighted her. During that period, a sonogram reevaluation showed that her ovarian cysts had completely disappeared. Sonia's menstrual cycle also returned to a normal twenty-eight-day monthly cycle, a necessary precursor to her hoped-for pregnancy. Although Sonia did not get pregnant, other patients of mine with a similar history were able to conceive.

Lisa's Story

Blood type O, female, 49

Lisa was at least 30 pounds above her ideal body weight. Her weight soared after her doctor prescribed prednisone for a serious lung disease. Lisa also had Lyme disease and was entering menopause.

I designed an eating regimen for Lisa based on her O blood type. I advised her to avoid wheat and dairy completely. Lisa learned what foods could be substituted, and she started to change her family's diet, replacing dairy with soy products and eating rice pasta instead of regular pasta.

To date, Lisa has lost 26 1/2 pounds and is motivated to lose the remaining 5 pounds. Lisa writes:

> The thing I noticed immediately was the amazing amount of energy I had after eliminating wheat and dairy. I don't remember when I'd felt better. Then the pounds started coming off. I've been on many diets but have never been able to stick to one for any length of time or would get to my goal weight only to find the pounds creeping back on again. The new foods taste so good that I don't have to cook different meals for my family. We are now all eating well-balanced, healthy meals. Dina's diet is really not a diet with a capital D. It's a way of eating that you can live with forever without feeling deprived. I never feel hungry nor do

I ever feel stuffed. The other wonderful discovery I made was that while people around me were getting sick with viruses and the flu, I managed to stay healthy. This eating style was also boosting my immunity.

Paula's Story

Blood type AB, female, 40

Paula weighed 204 pounds, had high blood pressure, and was suffering from frequent migraine headaches when she came to see me. She followed the AB food combining plan and in the first week lost 6 pounds. The second week she lost 5 pounds, and her energy level had increased significantly. Eliminating wheat and corn eased her headaches, and eventually she no longer had migraines at all. Paula didn't mind giving up wheat, because she was allowed to have wine two to three times a week with a protein meal and even two small squares of chocolate three times a week!

At our last meeting, she weighed 158 pounds and continues to very slowly drop weight. She looks great, and although her blood pressure did not drop significantly, many other things changed for the better. No more flatulence, no more migraines. Plus, her energy level has increased enormously. Paula found the program exceptionally easy to follow, and never feels deprived because she can eat almost anything (except wheat)—just not all at once.

Sharon's Story

Blood type B, female, 28

Sharon grew up being overweight, and she was constantly trying to find some miracle diet to make her thin. She was thirteen years old when she went to a Weight Watchers camp. She lost 20 pounds that summer, but after two months, she gained back the weight plus 10 more pounds. Next, she tried Slimfast, losing perhaps 5 pounds, but the weight always came back and then increased some more. Sharon moved on to the grapefruit diet and other fad diets, but they never worked. She decided to return to Weight Watchers and attended meetings for a few months. Though she lost weight, she was always hungry and was becoming highly discouraged. When she eventually stopped Weight Watchers, her weight rose to over 180 pounds. Sharon desperately needed to lose weight for an upcoming wedding. She tried the popular high-protein, low-carbohydrate diet and lost 20 pounds but could not lose any more.

About two years ago, and many pounds heavier, Sharon finally came to see me. I put her on the B blood type food combination diet. After the first month, Sharon lost 10 pounds and felt more energetic. In four and a half months, she lost 40 pounds and decided to start an exercise program to help her lose even more weight. Sharon started to cheat twice a month eating chocolate or ice cream. She was amazed when she gained only 1 or 2 pounds after these indiscretions. Before, if she went off her diet, she gained 7 to 10 pounds or more.

Sharon has maintained her current weight for two years and feels it is relatively easy because she eats what she wants and how much she wants. She doesn't have to worry about counting calories or measuring portion sizes. Most important of all, Sharon is learning how to be happy with who she is. Sharon writes:

> Since I came to see Dina and changed my eating patterns and food choices, I have noticed a dramatic positive change in my personality. I am not the angry, glum person I used to be. I smile more often. In fact, I have learned a great deal throughout this entire experience. The primary reason that this approach has worked so well is that I am losing weight *for me*. I also do not have to put a great deal of thought into meal planning. The only advice I have is to have the proper mental state to go through the process of losing weight and be willing to give it time to work.

CHAPTER THREE

The
Specifics

The weight-loss meals in this chapter, which are based on food combining principles and blood type theory, are designed to help you follow the program easily. The food combining charts for each blood type will show you how to properly combine your foods.

The food lists are arranged as to how frequently a food should be eaten:

- *Frequent* foods can be eaten as often as you wish.

- *Occasional* foods are best limited to twice a week.

- *Seldom* foods are ideally restricted to no more than once every three months.

Depending on how much weight you need to lose, you can stay on the weight-loss menus for three months or longer. Most people will lose 1 to 3 pounds per week. The more weight you have to lose, the more pounds will be lost per week.

Whether you need to drop only 3 pounds or 120 pounds, you can benefit from this program. The weight-loss menu samples are for one week. *Please note that recipes are included in chapter 4 for meals marked with an asterisk (*).*

The sample maintenance menus that follow the weight-loss menus are designed to help maintain the weight that has been lost. Having only fresh fruit for breakfast is no longer necessary. Wheat-free starches can now be eaten at breakfast; combining protein and starches at a meal occasionally is also fine. If you are sensitive to carbohydrates and would prefer to restrict your intake, I suggest consuming only one starch meal per day. Breakfast, mid-afternoon snacks, and dinner are usually the best times to have a starch meal. Starches at lunchtime often make one feel drowsy and tired.

Many of you are not breakfast eaters. However, I strongly recommend at least fruit for breakfast. In the winter, I suggest eating warm, cooked fruit (e.g., baked or poached apples or pears) as this is more filling than cold fruit. Eating first thing in the morning gives the metabolism a jump start. If you are a breakfast eater, and fruit alone doesn't satisfy you or makes you even hungrier, I recommend eating wheat-free whole grains that you can combine with some protein. Nut butters, cheese (dairy or nondairy), and eggs can be combined with wheat-free breads or cereals.

For optimal weight loss, I usually recommend only one starch meal a day and one starch snack. For example, if you have a slice of toast for breakfast, don't eat starch for lunch and dinner. You can, however, have a starch snack mid-afternoon. Some of you may find that a protein-only breakfast is best for you. This is not recommended for those with kidney problems.

The best dinner meals are usually some kind of protein (e.g., meat, poultry, or fish) with vegetables and a salad. The vegetables can be lightly sautéed in oil and garlic. The portion size for dinner is usually 6 ounces of cooked protein. Once or twice a week, a starch meal, such as brown rice with stir-fried vegetables and tofu or legumes, can be eaten for dinner.

After a while, you will become familiar with which foods are compatible with each other—and you—and meal planning will become second nature. I know the menu ideas later in this chapter will help speed the process up a bit.

Snacks

It is best for dieters not to snack between breakfast and lunch, unless they have a blood-sugar imbalance. It is also best not to snack after dinner if you are trying to lose weight. The best time to snack is usually mid-afternoon, at least a couple of hours after lunch, or one to two hours before dinner.

The best snacks are:

- Fresh fruit
- Raw vegetables with allowed dip
- Rice crackers (not rice cakes)
- Spelt pretzels (unsalted)
- Wheat-free toast with nut butter
- Small handful of raw nuts
- Organic yogurt (for those eating dairy)
- Soup (vegetable-based or a broth)
- Dried fruits (e.g., prunes or apricots)
- Dark chocolate (small amount, e.g., two small squares)
- Wheat-free cookie or brownie (occasional, e.g., one or two times a week)
- Baked apple or pear (no added sugar)

Blood Type Food Lists and Menus

How to Determine Your Blood Type

If you do not know your blood type, there are many ways to find out. The simplest way is to donate blood, which is free. You can also ask your physician to type your blood while having other blood work done. If you have ever had major surgery, the hospital will often have records of your blood type. There are also home kits for blood typing. Finally, blood types are often included on birth or marriage certificates.

Blood Type O

Meats and Eggs* (Blood Type O)

Frequent	Occasional	Seldom
Beef	Chicken	Goose
Buffalo	Cornish hen	Pork and pork products
Lamb	Duck	
Liver	Eggs	
Veal	Ostrich	
Venison	Pheasant	
	Quail	
	Rabbit	
	Turkey	

Use organic meats and eggs whenever possible.

Fish and Shellfish (Blood Type O)

Frequent	Occasional	Seldom
Bluefish	Albacore tuna	Barracuda
Cod	Anchovy	Catfish
Halibut	Bass	Caviar
Herring	Calamari (squid)	Conch
Lemon sole	Clam	Lox
Mackerel	Crab	Octopus
Perch	Crayfish	Pickled herring
Pike	Eel	
Rainbow trout	Flounder	
Red snapper	Frog legs	
Salmon	Gray sole	
Sardines	Grouper	
Striped bass	Haddock	
Swordfish	Lobster	
White perch	Mahi-mahi	
Whitefish	Monkfish	
Yellowtail	Mussels	

Frequent	Occasional	Seldom
	Ocean perch	
	Oysters	
	Porgy	
	Sailfish	
	Scallops	
	Shark	
	Shrimp	
	Silver perch	
	Smelt	
	Snails	
	Turtle	

Dairy* (Blood Type O)

Frequent	Occasional	Seldom
	Butter	American cheese
	Farmer cheese	Blue cheese
	Feta cheese	Brie cheese
	Goat cheese	Buttermilk cheese
	Mozzarella cheese	Camembert cheese
	Soy cheese	Casein
	Soy milk	Cheddar cheese
		Colby cheese
		Cottage cheese
		Cream cheese
		Edam cheese
		Emmenthal cheese
		Goat milk
		Gouda cheese
		Gruyère cheese
		Ice cream
		Jarlsberg cheese
		Kefir
		Milk (cow's)

(continued)

Dairy* (Blood Type O) continued

Frequent	Occasional	Seldom
		Monterey Jack cheese
		Muenster cheese
		Parmesan cheese
		Provolone cheese
		Ricotta cheese
		Romano cheese
		String cheese
		Swiss cheese
		Whey
		All types of yogurt

* Wherever possible, select cheese made from organic raw milk. The enzymes present encourage efficient metabolism and have the least likelihood of affecting mucous membranes and sinuses.

Oils (Blood Type O)

Frequent	Occasional	Seldom
Extra virgin olive oil	Canola oil	Avocado
Flaxseed oil*	Cod liver oil	Corn oil
Grapeseed oil	Sesame oil	Cottonseed oil
	Soy oil	Margarine, all types
	Sunflower oil	Peanut oil
	Walnut oil	Safflower oil

*Do not cook with this oil.

Nuts and Seeds (Blood Type O)

Frequent	Occasional	Seldom
Pumpkin seeds (raw)	Almond butter (raw)	Brazil nuts
Walnuts	Almonds (raw)	Cashews
	Hazelnuts	Cashew butter
	Hickory nuts	Litchi nuts
	Macadamia nuts	Peanuts (organic)
	Pecans	Peanut butter (organic)

Frequent	Occasional	Seldom
	Pignoli nuts	Pistachios
	Sesame butter (raw)	Poppy seeds
	Sesame seeds (raw)	
	Soy nut butter (unhydrogenated)	
	Soy nuts (unsalted)	
	Sunflower butter	
	Sunflower seeds (raw)	

Beans (Blood Type O)

Frequent	Occasional	Seldom
Adzuki beans	Black beans	Kidney beans
Black-eyed peas	Broad beans	Lentils
Pinto beans	Cannellini beans	Navy beans
	Chickpeas (garbanzos)	Tamarind beans
	Fava beans	
	Great northern beans	
	Lima beans	
	Red soybeans	
	Tempeh	
	Tofu	

Grains (Blood Type O)

Frequent	Occasional	Seldom
Ezekiel bread	Amaranth	All bran products
Manna bread	Barley	Bagels
	Buckwheat	Bulgur
	Cream of rice	Cornflakes
	Ezekiel bagels*	Corn products
	Kasha	Cream of Wheat
	Millet	Grape-Nuts
	Oat bran	Semolina products
	Oatmeal	Shredded Wheat
	Rice bran	White flour

(continued)

Grains (Blood Type O) *continued*

Frequent	Occasional	Seldom
	Rice crackers	Whole wheat flour
	100% rye bread	
	100% rye crackers	
	Spelt products	
	Wheat-free bread	

* Ezekiel brand bagels have less fiber than Ezekiel bread. Hypoglycemics and diabetics may do better with Ezekiel bread, which is also better for weight loss.

Starchy Vegetables (Blood Type O)

Frequent	Occasional	Seldom
Artichokes	Acorn squash	Avocados
Parsnips	Beets	Corn
Pumpkin	Butternut squash	Potatoes (white)
Sweet potatoes	Chestnuts	
	Rutabaga	
	Spaghetti squash	
	Yams	

Low-Starch Vegetables (Blood Type O)

Frequent	Occasional	Seldom
Beet greens	Arugula	Alfalfa sprouts
Broccoli	Asparagus	Brussels sprouts
Broccoli rabe	Celery	Cauliflower
Collard greens	Coriander	Eggplant
Dandelion greens	Cucumber	Mushrooms (white,
Escarole	Daikon	shiitake)
Garlic	Dill	Mustard greens
Horseradish	Endive	Olives (black, Greek,
Kale	Fennel	Spanish)
Kohlrabi	Ferns	
Leek	Ginger	
Lettuce, romaine	Lettuce (Bibb, Boston,	
Okra	iceberg, mesclun)	

Frequent	Occasional	Seldom
Onions	Mushrooms	
Parsley	(Portobello or wild)	
Parsnips	Olives (green)	
Peppers (red)	Peppers (green,	
Seaweed	jalapeño, yellow)	
Spinach	Radicchio	
Swiss chard	Radishes	
Turnips	Rutabaga	
	Scallions	
	Shallots	
	Snow peas	
	Sprouts (mung, radish)	
	Tomatoes	
	Water chestnuts	
	Watercress	
	Zucchini	

Fresh Fruits and Juices* (Blood Type O)

Frequent	Occasional	Seldom
Black cherry juice	Apples (fresh or dried)	Apple juice and cider
Figs (best are black	Apricots (fresh or	Bananas
mission)	unsulphured)	Blackberries
Pineapple	Blueberries	Cantaloupe
Plums	Cherries	Honeydew
Prunes	Cranberries	Orange juice
Prune juice	Crenshaw melon	Rhubarb
	Currants	Strawberries
	Dates	Tangerines
	Grapefruit	
	Grapes	
	Guava	
	Kiwis	
	Kumquat	
	Lemons	
	Limes	
	Mango (fresh or dried)	*(continued)*

Frequent	Occasional	Seldom
	Nectarines	
	Papaya	
	Peaches (fresh or dried)	
	Pears (fresh or dried)	
	Persian melon	
	Persimmon	
	Pineapple	
	Pomegranate	
	Raisins	
	Raspberries	
	Star fruit	
	Watermelon	

Juices, in general, are not recommended for weight loss unless freshly squeezed. Only organic fresh fruit and unsweetened juices are recommended.

Beverages (Blood Type O)

Frequent	Occasional	Seldom
Cayenne tea	Beer*	Alfalfa tea
Dandelion tea	Chamomile tea	Aloe vera tea
Fenugreek tea	Dong quai tea	Black tea (all types)
Ginger tea	Elder tea	Burdock tea
Green tea	Ginseng tea	Coffee (all types)
Linden tea	Hawthorne tea	Corn silk tea
Mint tea	Licorice tea	Echinacea tea
Parsley tea	Raspberry leaf tea	Goldenseal tea
Rose hips tea	Valerian tea	Liquor (all types)*
Seltzer	Vervain tea	Red clover tea
Slippery elm tea	Wine (all types)*	Rhubarb tea
		St. John's wort tea
		Senna tea
		Soda (all types)
		Strawberry leaf tea
		Yellow dock tea

If you do not drink alcohol, please do not take this recommendation as an encouragement to start drinking.

Food Combining Chart: Blood Type O

Proteins*

Adzuki beans	Rabbit
Pinto beans	Calf's liver
Split peas	Organic eggs
Tofu	Goat cheese
Venison	
Lamb	

Turkey
Fish
Shellfish
Organic chicken
Organic beef
Buffalo

*Eat only one protein food at a meal.

GOOD TO COMBINE

POOR TO COMBINE

Starches

Chestnuts	Butternut squash
Pumpkin	Frozen peas
Millet	Amaranth
Ezekiel bread	Cereal/grains (wheat-free)
Cooked carrots	Artichokes
Acorn squash	

Brown rice
Beets
Yams
Parsnips
Spelt
Potatoes

GOOD TO COMBINE

Green and Low-Starch Vegetables

Zucchini	Endive
String beans	Onions
Snow peas	Lettuce
Kohlrabi	Fennel
Portobello mushrooms	Radicchio

Red peppers
Spinach
Asparagus
Cucumber
Broccoli

Fresh peas
Sugar snap peas
Collard greens
Turnips
Garlic

Kale
Mung bean sprouts
Watercress
Escarole
Arugula

Fats and Oils (combine with protein or starch)

Walnuts
Olive oil

Grapeseed oil
Raw almonds

Soy margarine*
Mayonnaise

Raw almond butter
Raw pumpkin seeds

Organic butter (small quantity)

*Use unhydrogenated margarine.

POOR TO COMBINE

Sweet Fruits

Fresh figs
Fresh dates
Grapes (purple, black)

Sapote
Prunes
Papaya

POOR TO COMBINE

Sub-Acid Fruits

Plums	Apricots
Mangoes	Apples
Pears	Nectarines
Berries	Cherries
Peaches	Green grapes

POOR TO COMBINE

Acid Fruits

Lemons	Kiwis
Grapefruit	Pomegranate
Limes	Kumquats
Pineapple	Cranberries

Melons (poor to combine / eat alone)

Crenshaw   Watermelon

One Week of Sample Weight-Loss Menus for Blood Type O

Day 1

Breakfast: 1 slice Ezekiel toast with raw almond butter. (Those who are not breakfast eaters may choose fresh fruit instead. See the table on page 29 for allowed fruits.)

Lunch: Salmon salad and spinach salad

Dinner: Organic steak with curried greens and turnips

Day 2

Breakfast: 1 slice Ezekiel toast with organic butter and plum butter

Lunch: 4 ounces organic roast beef over mixed greens

Dinner: Baked cod with Swiss chard and a tossed salad

Day 3

Breakfast: 1 slice Ezekiel toast with tofu cream cheese

Lunch: 4 ounces organic roast beef plus a large green salad

Dinner: Lamb chops with asparagus and string beans

Day 4

Breakfast: 1 slice spelt toast topped with 1 poached egg

Lunch: Hamburger with sautéed vegetables

Dinner: Swordfish steak with broccoli and snow peas

Day 5

Breakfast: 1 slice spelt toast and goat cheese

Lunch: Grilled chicken or shrimp Caesar Salad

Dinner: Calf's liver with onions and sautéed spinach and turnips

Day 6

Breakfast: 1 slice spelt toast and raw sesame butter

Lunch: Sardines in a spinach salad

Dinner: Baked salmon with lemon broccoli rabe and grilled peppers

Day 7

Breakfast: 1 slice Ezekiel toast topped with 1 poached egg

Lunch: Turkey breast with mixed greens

Dinner: Veal cutlets sautéed with Portobello mushrooms and string beans

Sample Maintenance Menus for Blood Type O

Day 1

Breakfast: $^1/_2$ Ezekiel bagel and 2 veal or lamb sausages

Lunch: Tuna salad with a large green salad

Dinner: Calf's liver and onions with sautéed spinach and sweet potatoes

Day 2

Breakfast: Cream of brown rice cereal and soy milk. (Sprinkle flax meal or flax powder on the cereal to add extra fiber.)

Lunch: Grilled hamburger with onions and sautéed vegetables

Dinner: Seafood stir-fry with vegetables

Day 3

Breakfast: 1 slice Ezekiel toast and 2 eggs, any style

Lunch: Organic roast beef sandwich on spelt or Ezekiel bread with a tossed salad

Dinner: Pinto beans with sautéed escarole over $^1/_2$ cup brown rice

Day 4

Breakfast: 1 or 2 slices Ezekiel toast with raw almond butter

Lunch: Shrimp or salmon Caesar Salad*

Dinner: Vegetable rice lasagna and a green salad

Day 5

Breakfast: 1 or 2 slices Ezekiel toast with raw sesame butter and fruit juice–sweetened jam

Lunch: Salmon salad over mixed greens

Dinner: Lamb chops with grilled vegetable kabobs

Day 6

Breakfast: 1 or 2 slices Ezekiel toast with fresh goat cheese

Lunch: Chicken salad with a spinach salad

Dinner: Halibut roasted in pesto with roasted vegetables

Day 7

Breakfast: 1 cup spelt flakes with 1 cup soy milk

Lunch: Sardines with marinated string beans and Fennel Broccoli Slaw*

Dinner: Organic steak with steamed broccoli and baked sweet potato fries

Recipe is included in recipe section.

Blood Type A

Meats and Eggs* (Blood Type A)

Frequent	Occasional	Seldom
	Chicken	Beef
	Eggs	Buffalo
	Cornish hen	Duck
	Turkey	Goose
		Lamb
		Liver
		Ostrich
		Pheasant
		Pork and pork products
		Quail
		Rabbit
		Veal
		Venison

*Use organic meats and eggs whenever possible.

Fish and Shellfish (Blood Type A)

Frequent	Occasional	Seldom
Cod	Albacore tuna	Anchovies
Grouper	Mahi-mahi	Barracuda
Mackerel	Pike	Bluefish
Monkfish	Porgy	Calamari (squid)
Perch	Sea bass	Catfish
Rainbow trout	Shark	Caviar
Red snapper	Smelts	Clams
Salmon	Swordfish	Conch
Sardines	Yellowtail	Crab
Sea trout		Crayfish
Snails (escargots)		Eel
Whitefish		Flounder
		Frog legs

(continued)

Fish and Shellfish (Blood Type A) *continued*

Frequent	Occasional	Seldom
		Haddock
		Halibut
		Herring
		Lobster
		Lox
		Mussels
		Octopus
		Oysters
		Scallops
		Shrimp
		Sole
		Striped bass

Dairy* (Blood Type A)

Frequent	Occasional	Seldom
Canola oil margarine**	Farmer cheese	American cheese
Soy cheese	Feta cheese	Blue cheese
Soy margarine**	Goat cheese	Brie cheese
Soy milk	Goat's milk	Butter
Tofu cream cheese	Kefir	Buttermilk
	Mozzarella cheese (fresh)	Camembert cheese
	Ricotta cheese	Casein
	String cheese	Cheddar cheese
	Yogurt (plain, with fruit, frozen)	Colby cheese
		Cottage cheese
		Cream cheese
		Edam cheese
		Gouda cheese
		Gruyère cheese
		Havarti cheese
		Ice cream
		Jarlsberg cheese

Frequent	Occasional	Seldom
		Milk (cow's)
		Monterey Jack cheese
		Muenster cheese
		Parmesan cheese
		Provolone cheese
		Romano cheese
		Sherbet
		Swiss cheese
		Whey

* *Wherever possible, select cheese made from organic raw milk. The enzymes present encourage efficient metabolism and have the least likelihood of affecting mucous membranes and sinuses.*
** *Use unhydrogenated margarine.*

Oils (Blood Type A)

Frequent	Occasional	Seldom
Extra virgin olive oil	Avocado	Corn oil
Flaxseed oil*	Canola oil	Cottonseed oil
Grapeseed oil	Soy oil	Peanut oil
	Sunflower oil	Safflower oil
	Walnut oil	Sesame oil

Do not cook with this oil.

Nuts and Seeds (Blood Type A)

Frequent	Occasional	Seldom
Peanut butter (organic)	Almond butter (raw)	Brazil nuts
Peanuts in the shell (unsalted)	Almonds (raw)	Cashews
Pumpkin seeds (raw)	Hazelnut butter	Pistachios
Soy nut butter	Hazelnuts	
Soy nuts (unsalted)	Hickory	
	Macadamia nuts	
	Pignoli nuts	
	Poppy seeds	*(continued)*

Nuts and Seeds (Blood Type A) *continued*

Frequent	Occasional	Seldom
	Sesame seeds (raw)	
	Sunflower butter	
	Sunflower seeds (raw)	
	Walnuts	

Beans (Blood Type A)

Frequent	Occasional	Seldom
Adzuki beans	Broad beans	Chickpeas (garbanzos)
Black beans	Cannellini beans	Kidney beans
Black-eyed peas	Fava beans	Lima beans
Lentils	White beans	Navy beans
Pinto beans		Red chili beans
Soybeans		Tamarind beans
Tempeh		
Tofu		

Grains (Blood Type A)

Frequent	Occasional	Seldom
Amaranth	Artichoke pasta	Bulgur
Buckwheat	Bagels	Couscous
Ezekiel bread	Barley	Cream of Wheat
Kasha	Corn products	Familia muesli
Manna bread	Cornflakes	Grape-Nuts
Oat flour	Cream of rice	Multigrain products
Rice flour	Ezekiel bagels*	Pumpernickel
Rye flour	Kamut	Semolina pasta
Soba noodles	Millet	Seven-grain products
Soy flour	Oat bran	Shredded Wheat
	Oatmeal	White flour
	Quinoa	Whole wheat products**

Frequent	Occasional	Seldom
	Rice	
	Rice bran	
	100% rye bread	
	Rye crackers	
	Spelt	

* Ezekiel brand bagels have less fiber than Ezekiel bread. Hypoglycemics and diabetics may do better with Ezekiel bread, which is also better for weight loss.

**Avoid whole wheat products to lose weight and/or if you have any medical conditions such as allergies, asthma, arthritis, cancer, and others.

Starchy Vegetables (Blood Type A)

Frequent	Occasional	Seldom
Artichokes	Acorn squash	Potatoes
Parsnips	Butternut squash	Sweet potatoes
Pumpkin	Corn on the cob	Yams
	Spaghetti squash	

Low-Starch Vegetables (Blood Type A)

Frequent	Occasional	Seldom
Alfalfa sprouts	Arugula	Cabbage
Beet greens	Asparagus	Eggplant
Broccoli	Bamboo shoots	Lima beans
Carrots	Beets	Mushrooms (shiitake,
Collard greens	Bok choy	white)
Dandelion greens	Brussels sprouts	Olives (black)
Escarole	Cauliflower	Peppers (all types)
Garlic	Celery	Tomatoes
Horseradish	Coriander	
Kale	Cucumber	
Kohlrabi	Daikon radish	
Leek	Endive	
Okra	Fennel	
Onions	Ferns	*(continued)*

Low-Starch Vegetables (Blood Type A) *continued*

Frequent	Occasional	Seldom
Parsley	Lettuce (Boston, Bibb,	
Romaine lettuce	red leaf, green leaf)	
Spinach	Mesclun mix	
Swiss chard	Mung bean sprouts	
Turnips	Mustard greens	
	Olives (green)	
	Portobello mushrooms	
	Radicchio	
	Radishes	
	Scallions	
	Seaweed	
	Shallots	
	Water chestnuts	
	Watercress	
	Wild mushrooms	
	Zucchini	

Fresh Fruits and Juices* (Blood Type A)

Frequent	Occasional	Seldom
Apricot juice	Apple juice and cider	Bananas
Apricots	Apples	Cantaloupe
Black cherry juice	Cabbage juice	Coconut
Blackberries	Cranberry juice	Honeydew
Blueberries	Crenshaw melon	Mango
Carrot juice	Cucumber juice	Orange juice
Celery juice	Currants	Oranges
Cherries	Dates	Papaya
Cranberries	Grapes	Papaya juice
Figs (black mission)	Grape juice	Rhubarb
Grapefruit	Guava	Tangerines
Grapefruit juice	Kiwis	Tomato juice
Lemons	Limes	
Pineapple	Nectarines	

Frequent	Occasional	Seldom
Pineapple juice	Peaches	
Plums	Pears	
Prune juice	Persian melon	
Prunes	Persimmons	
Raisins	Pomegranate	
	Raspberries	
	Star fruit	
	Strawberries	
	Watermelon	

Juices, in general, are not recommended for weight loss unless freshly squeezed. Only organic fresh fruit and unsweetened juices are recommended.

Beverages** (Blood Type A)

Frequent	Occasional	Seldom
Alfalfa tea	Coltsfoot tea	Beer*
Aloe vera tea	Dandelion tea	Black tea
Burdock tea	Dong quai tea	Carbonated sodas
Chamomile tea	Gentian tea	(all types)
Coffee (organic)	Goldenseal tea	Carbonated water
Detox tea	Licorice root tea	Corn silk tea
Echinacea tea	Linden tea	Liquor (all types)*
Fenugreek tea	Mint tea	Rhubarb tea
Ginger tea	Parsley tea	
Ginseng tea	Raspberry leaf tea	
Green tea	Red clover tea	
Hawthorn tea	Senna tea	
Milk thistle tea	Strawberry leaf tea	
Red wine*	White wine*	
Rose hips tea		
St. John's wort tea		
Slippery elm tea		
Valerian tea		

* If you do not drink alcohol, please do not take this recommendation as an encouragement to start drinking.

** Whenever possible, make sure teas are herbal.

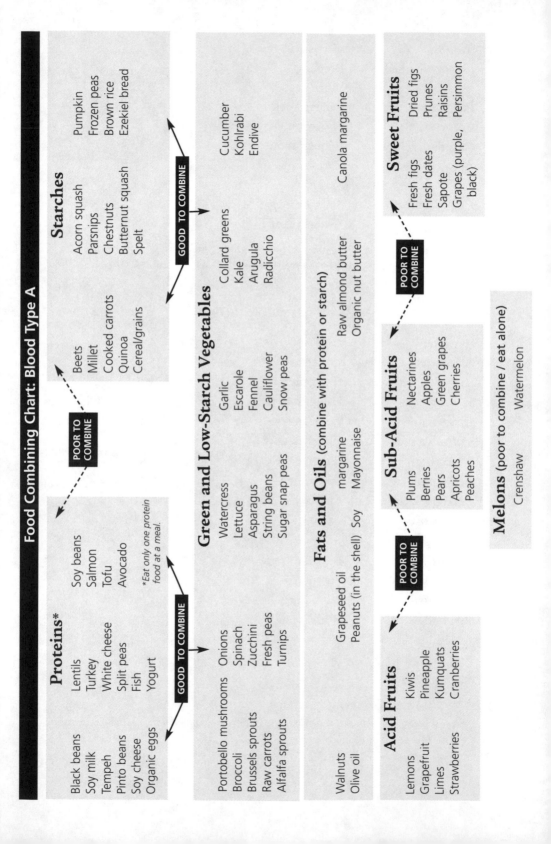

Food Combining Chart: Blood Type A

Proteins*

Black beans
Soy milk
Tempeh
Pinto beans
Soy cheese
Organic eggs

Lentils
Turkey
White cheese
Split peas
Fish
Yogurt

Soy beans
Salmon
Tofu
Avocado

*Eat only one protein food at a meal.

Starches

Beets
Millet
Cooked carrots
Quinoa
Cereal/grains

Acorn squash
Parsnips
Chestnuts
Butternut squash
Spelt

Pumpkin
Frozen peas
Brown rice
Ezekiel bread

POOR TO COMBINE

GOOD TO COMBINE

Green and Low-Starch Vegetables

Portobello mushrooms
Broccoli
Brussels sprouts
Raw carrots
Alfalfa sprouts

Onions
Spinach
Zucchini
Fresh peas
Turnips

Watercress
Lettuce
Asparagus
String beans
Sugar snap peas

Garlic
Escarole
Fennel
Cauliflower
Snow peas

Collard greens
Kale
Arugula
Radicchio

Cucumber
Kohlrabi
Endive

GOOD TO COMBINE

Fats and Oils (combine with protein or starch)

Walnuts
Olive oil

Grapeseed oil
Peanuts (in the shell) Soy

margarine
Mayonnaise

Raw almond butter
Organic nut butter

Canola margarine

Acid Fruits

Lemons
Grapefruit
Limes
Strawberries

Kiwis
Pineapple
Kumquats
Cranberries

POOR TO COMBINE

Sub-Acid Fruits

Plums
Berries
Pears
Apricots
Peaches

Nectarines
Apples
Green grapes
Cherries

POOR TO COMBINE

Sweet Fruits

Fresh figs
Fresh dates
Sapote
Grapes (purple, black)

Dried figs
Prunes
Raisins
Persimmon

Melons (poor to combine / eat alone)

Crenshaw   Watermelon

One Week of Sample Weight-Loss Menus for Blood Type A

Day 1

Breakfast: Fresh pineapple, kiwis, and strawberries
Lunch: Lentil soup with 1 slice Ezekiel toast and a small salad
Dinner: Codfish Salad* with sautéed greens

Day 2

Breakfast: Watermelon
Lunch: 6 ounces tuna with a large green salad
Dinner: 1 cup pinto beans with ¹/₂ cup brown or wild rice and
    steamed greens

Day 3

Breakfast: Pears and apples
Lunch: 6 ounces grilled turkey Caesar Salad*
Dinner: Red snapper with broccoli or String Beans with Shallots* and
    a tossed salad

Day 4

Breakfast: Grapes
Lunch: Black bean soup with 1 slice Ezekiel toast and a small tossed salad
Dinner: Turkey burger with sautéed spinach and a mixed green salad

Day 5

Breakfast: Grapefruit and strawberries
Lunch: 6 ounces salmon with a spinach salad
Dinner: Baked cod with Swiss chard and turnips

Day 6

Breakfast: Blueberries and raspberries
Lunch: Tofu and stir-fried veggies
Dinner: Trout with asparagus and mixed greens

Day 7

Breakfast: Plums
Lunch: Sardines with a mixed green salad
Dinner: Roasted Chicken with Herbs* with veggies and salad

Sample Maintenance Menus for Blood Type A

Day 1

Breakfast: 1 cup oatmeal cooked in 1 cup soy milk
Lunch: Miso soup with tofu and cucumber sushi rolls
Dinner: Pinto beans sautéed with onions and spinach over kasha (buckwheat groats)

Day 2

Breakfast: Amaranth flakes with soy milk
Lunch: Black bean salad with cold noodle salad
Dinner: Roasted Chicken with Herbs* with vegetable ragout

Day 3

Breakfast: 1 or 2 slices Ezekiel bread with organic peanut butter
Lunch: Lentil soup with 1 slice Ezekiel toast
Dinner: Fresh salmon baked with grilled vegetable kabobs

Day 4

Breakfast: Ezekiel bagel with raw almond butter
Lunch: Tuna salad on wheat-free bread plus raw vegetable sticks
Dinner: Red snapper in a curry sauce over millet and marinated string beans

Day 5

Breakfast: Ezekiel bagel with tofu cream cheese
Lunch: Turkey breast with a Caesar Salad*
Dinner: Make your own pizza plus a green salad

Day 6

Breakfast: 2 buckwheat pancakes with pure maple syrup or any fruit-sweetened jam

Lunch: Boca burger on a spelt roll with a green salad

Dinner: Turkey meatballs in pesto over rice spaghetti or artichoke pasta

Day 7

Breakfast: ³/₄ cup wheat-free granola and soy milk

Lunch: Salmon patties and a spinach salad

Dinner: Spelt spaghetti with vegetable primavera

* Recipe is included in recipe section.

Blood Type B

Meats and Eggs* (Blood Type B)

Frequent	Occasional	Seldom
Eggs	Beef	Chicken
Lamb	Buffalo	Cornish hen
Rabbit	Calf's liver	Duck
Venison	Pheasant	Goose
	Turkey	Pork and pork products
	Veal	Quail

* Use organic meats and eggs whenever possible.

Fish and Shellfish (Blood Type B)

Frequent	Occasional	Seldom
Cod	Albacore tuna	Anchovies
Flounder	Bluefish	Barracuda
Grouper	Calamari (squid)	Clams
Haddock	Catfish	Conch
Halibut	Herring	Crab
Mackerel	Perch (freshwater)	Crayfish
		(continued)

Fish and Shellfish (Blood Type B) *continued*

Frequent	Occasional	Seldom
Mahi-mahi	Rainbow trout	Eel
Monkfish	Red snapper	Frog legs
Perch (saltwater)	Scallops	Lobster
Pike	Shark	Lox
Sardines	Smelts	Mussels
Sea trout	Swordfish	Octopus
Sole	Whitefish	Oysters
		Sea bass
		Shrimp
		Snails
		Striped bass
		Yellowtail

Dairy* (Blood Type B)

Frequent	Occasional	Seldom
Cottage cheese	Brie cheese	American cheese
Farmer cheese	Butter	Blue cheese
Feta cheese	Buttermilk	Ice cream
Goat cheese	Camembert cheese	String cheese
Goat milk	Cheddar cheese	
Kefir	Colby cheese	
Milk (cow's; skim	Cream cheese	
or low-fat)	Edam cheese	
Mozzarella cheese	Gouda cheese	
(fresh)	Gruyère cheese	
Ricotta cheese	Jarlsberg cheese	
Yogurt (organic,	Monterey Jack cheese	
plain)	Muenster cheese	
	Parmesan cheese	
	Provolone cheese	
	Romano cheese	
	Sherbet	

Frequent	Occasional	Seldom
	Soy products (no tofu)	
	Swiss cheese	
	Whey	
	Whole milk (cow's)	
	Yogurt (frozen)	

Wherever possible, select cheese made from organic raw milk. The enzymes present encourage efficient metabolism and have the least likelihood of affecting mucous membranes and sinuses.

Oils (Blood Type B)

Frequent	Occasional	Seldom
Extra virgin olive oil	Cod liver oil	Avocado
Grapeseed oil	Flaxseed oil*	Canola oil
		Corn oil
		Cottonseed oil
		Peanut oil
		Safflower oil
		Sesame oil
		Sunflower oil

Do not cook with this oil.

Nuts and Seeds (Blood Type B)

Frequent	Occasional	Seldom
None	Almond butter (raw)	Cashews
	Almonds (raw)	Hazelnuts
	Brazil nuts	Hazelnut butter
	Litchi nuts	Peanuts (organic)
	Macadamia nuts	Peanut butter (organic)
	Pecans	Pignoli nuts
	Soy nuts	Pistachios
	Walnuts	Poppy seeds
		Pumpkin seeds

(continued)

Nuts and Seeds (Blood Type B) *continued*

Frequent	Occasional	Seldom
		Sesame butter
		Sesame seeds (raw)
		Sunflower butter
		Sunflower seeds (raw)

Beans (Blood Type B)

Frequent	Occasional	Seldom
Kidney beans	Broad beans	Adzuki beans
Lima beans	Cannellini beans	Black beans
Navy beans	Fava beans	Black-eyed peas
	Great northern beans	Chickpeas (garbanzos)
	Red beans	Lentils
	Split peas	Pinto beans
	Tamarind beans	Tempeh
	White beans	Tofu

Grains (Blood Type B)

Frequent	Occasional	Seldom
Ezekiel bread	Cream of rice	Amaranth
Manna bread	Ezekiel bagels*	Artichoke pasta
Millet	Granola	Bagels
Oat bran	Grape-Nuts	Barley
Oat flour	Muesli cereal	Buckwheat
Oatmeal	Pumpernickel	Bulgur
Rice bran	Quinoa	Corn products
Rice crackers (not	Rice (all types except	Couscous
rice cakes)	wild)	Cream of Wheat
Rice flour	Rye bread	Kamut
Spelt	Rye crackers	Kasha
	Semolina pasta	Multigrain products
	Spinach pasta	Shredded Wheat

Frequent	Occasional	Seldom
	White flour	Wheat bran
		Wheat germ
		Wild rice

* *Ezekiel brand bagels have less fiber than Ezekiel bread. Hypoglycemics and diabetics may do better with Ezekiel bread, which is also better for weight loss.*

Starchy Vegetables (Blood Type B)

Frequent	Occasional	Seldom
Beets	Acorn squash	Artichokes
Parsnips	Butternut squash	Chestnuts
Sweet potatoes	Peas, frozen	Corn on the cob
Yams	Rutabaga	Pumpkin
	Spaghetti squash	

Low-Starch Vegetables (Blood Type B)

Frequent	Occasional	Seldom
Beet greens	Alfalfa sprouts	Mung bean sprouts
Broccoli	Arugula	Olives
Brussels sprouts	Asparagus	Radishes
Cabbage	Bamboo shoots	Radish sprouts
Carrots	Bok choy	Tomatoes
Cauliflower	Celery	
Collard greens	Chicory	
Eggplant	Cucumber	
Kale	Daikon	
Mushrooms	Dandelion	
(shiitake)	Dill	
Mustard greens	Endive	
Parsley	Escarole	
Peppers	Fennel	
	Ferns	
	Garlic	

(continued)

Low-Starch Vegetables (Blood Type B) *continued*

Frequent	Occasional	Seldom
	Ginger	
	Horseradish	
	Kohlrabi	
	Leek	
	Mesclun mix	
	Okra	
	Onions	
	Portobello mushrooms	
	Radicchio	
	Romaine lettuce	
	Scallions	
	Seaweed	
	Snow peas	
	Spinach	
	String beans	
	Swiss chard	
	Turnips	
	Water chestnuts	
	Watercress	
	Zucchini	

Fresh Fruits and Juices* (Blood Type B)

Frequent	Occasional	Seldom
Bananas	Apple juice and cider	Persimmons
Cabbage juice	Apples	Pomegranate
Cranberries	Blackberries	Prickly pear
Cranberry juice	Blueberries	Rhubarb
Grape juice	Carrot juice	Star fruit
Grapes	Celery juice	Tomato juice
Papaya	Cherries	
Papaya juice	Cherry juice	
Pineapple	Cucumber juice	

Frequent	Occasional	Seldom
Pineapple juice	Currants	
Plums	Dates	
	Figs	
	Gooseberries	
	Grapefruit	
	Grapefruit juice	
	Guava	
	Kumquats	
	Limes	
	Mangoes	
	Melon	
	Nectarines	
	Orange juice	
	Oranges	
	Peaches	
	Pears	
	Prune juice	
	Prunes	
	Raisins	
	Raspberries	
	Strawberries	
	Tangerines	

Juices, in general, are not recommended for weight loss unless freshly squeezed. Only organic fresh fruit and unsweetened juices are recommended.

Beverages (Blood Type B)

Frequent	Occasional	Seldom
Ginger tea	Alfalfa tea	Aloe vera tea
Ginseng tea	Beer*	Coltsfoot tea
Green tea (Sencha)	Black tea	Corn silk tea
Licorice tea	Burdock tea	Fenugreek tea
Parsley tea	Chamomile tea	Gentian tea
Peppermint tea	Coffee (organic)	Linden tea
Raspberry leaf tea	Dandelion tea	Liquor (all types)*

(continued)

Frequent	Occasional	Seldom
Rose hips tea	Dong quai tea	Red clover tea
	Echinacea tea	Rhubarb tea
	Goldenseal tea	Seltzer
	Hawthorn tea	Senna tea
	Mint tea	Sodas (all types)
	St. John's wort tea	
	Slippery elm bark tea	
	Strawberry leaf tea	
	Valerian tea	
	Wine*	

* If you do not drink alcohol, please do not take this recommendation as an encouragement to start drinking.

One Week of Weight-Loss Menus for Blood Type B

Day 1

Breakfast: Fresh pineapple, kiwis, and strawberries
Lunch: Mock Greek Salad*
Dinner: Lamb chops with curried greens

Day 2

Breakfast: Fresh papaya
Lunch: Egg salad and a spinach salad
Dinner: Baked cod with Garlic Escarole*

Day 3

Breakfast: Watermelon
Lunch: Kidney beans with a mixed green salad
Dinner: Monkfish with snow peas and red peppers

Food Combining Chart: Blood Type B

Proteins*

Navy beans	Venison	Scallops
Split peas	Buffalo	White cheese
Kidney beans	Turkey	Calamari
Cannellini beans	Organic 1% milk	Yogurt
Lamb	Fish	Calf's liver
Rabbit	Organic eggs	*Eat only one protein food at a meal.

POOR TO COMBINE

Starches

Brown rice	Yams	Spelt
Potatoes	Ezekiel bread	Lima beans
Cooked carrots	Butternut squash	Oat bran
Beets	Parsnips	Cereal grains
Millet	Rice pasta	(wheat-free)
Acorn squash	Frozen peas	

GOOD TO COMBINE

Green and Low-Starch Vegetables

Cabbage	Onions	Watercress	Garlic	Collard greens	Kohlrabi
Broccoli	Spinach	Bok choy	Escarole	Kale	Peppers
Brussels sprouts	Zucchini	Asparagus	Lettuce	Arugula	Raw carrots
Eggplant	Fresh peas	String beans	Cauliflower	Fennel	Endive
Alfalfa sprouts	Turnips	Sugar snap peas	Snow peas	Cucumber	Mushrooms

GOOD TO COMBINE

Fats and Oils (combine with protein or starch)

Walnuts	Grapeseed oil	Raw almond butter	Mayonnaise	Organic sweet butter
Olive oil	Raw almonds			

Acid Fruits

Lemons	Kiwis
Grapefruit	Pineapple
Limes	Kumquats
Strawberries	Cranberries

POOR TO COMBINE

Sub-Acid Fruits

Plums	Apricots
Mangoes	Apples
Pears	Nectarines
Berries	Cherries
Peaches	Green grapes

POOR TO COMBINE

Sweet Fruits

Bananas*	Papaya
Fresh figs	Sapote
Fresh dates	Dried figs
Grapes (purple, black)	Prunes
	*Limit for weight loss.

Melons (poor to combine / eat alone)

Crenshaw   Honeydew   Cantaloupe   Watermelon

Day 4

Breakfast: Blueberries and raspberries (in season). If unavailable, choose apples, grapes, or pears.
Lunch: Grilled turkey Caesar Salad*
Dinner: Baked yam with stir-fried vegetables

Day 5

Breakfast: Grapes
Lunch: Fresh mozzarella cheese with basil, roasted peppers, and spinach
Dinner: Turkey Cutlets with Lemon and Garlic Escarole*

Day 6

Breakfast: Plums
Lunch: Sardines on Ezekiel bread and raw vegetables
Dinner: Cannellini beans sautéed with garlic, onions, and escarole

Day 7

Breakfast: Cantaloupe
Lunch: Split pea soup and a tossed salad
Dinner: Calf's liver and onions with broccoli and turnips

Recipe is included in recipe section.

Sample Maintenance Menus for Blood Type B

Day 1

Breakfast: Low-fat organic plain yogurt with berries
Lunch: Turkey burger on spelt roll (optional) and coleslaw
Dinner: Spelt spaghetti with grilled vegetable kabobs

Day 2

Breakfast: 1 or 2 slices yeast-free spelt toast with low-fat goat cheese
Lunch: 3/4 cup kidney beans with Fennel Slaw*
Dinner: Lamb chops with marinated string beans and 1/2 roasted yam, Cajun-style

Day 3

Breakfast: 1/2 cup oatmeal cooked in 1 cup organic 1% milk
Lunch: Organic roast beef slices with mustard and lettuce on Ezekiel bread
Dinner: Baked halibut and stir-fried vegetables

Day 4

Breakfast: 1 or 2 slices yeast-free spelt toast with 2 or 3 ounces feta cheese
Lunch: Spinach omelets with a green salad and 1 slice Ezekiel bread
Dinner: Sautéed liver and onions with escarole and roasted yams

Day 5

Breakfast: 1 cup 100% oat bran flakes with 1 cup organic 1% milk
Lunch: Sardines (or any fish) in marinated Japanese vegetable salad
Dinner: Vegetable cheese lasagna with a Caesar Salad*

Day 6

Breakfast: 1 or 2 slices Ezekiel toast with 2 eggs, any style
Lunch: Organic turkey breast slices on an Ezekiel bagel with a green salad
Dinner: Curried rice noodles (Ma Fun) and vegetable primavera

Day 7

Breakfast: Ezekiel bagel with low-fat or regular organic cream cheese
Lunch: 4 ounces fresh mozzarella cheese on 2 slices wheat-free bread with marinated roast peppers and basil
Dinner: Grilled mahi-mahi with pesto sauce and broccoli sautéed in olive oil and garlic

Recipe is included in recipe section.

Blood Type AB

Meats and Eggs* (Blood Type AB)

Frequent	Occasional	Seldom
Eggs	Liver	Beef
Lamb	Pheasant	Buffalo
Rabbit		Chicken
Turkey		Cornish hen
		Duck
		Goose
		Pork and pork products
		Quail
		Veal
		Venison

Use organic meats and eggs whenever possible.

Fish and Shellfish (Blood Type AB)

Frequent	Occasional	Seldom
Albacore tuna	Bluefish	Anchovies
Cod	Calamari (squid)	Barracuda
Grouper	Catfish	Clams
Hake	Caviar	Conch
Mackerel	Fresh herring	Crab
Mahi-mahi	Mussels	Crayfish
Monkfish	Scallops	Eel
Perch (ocean)	Shark	Flounder
Pike	Smelts	Frog legs
Rainbow trout	Sole	Gray sole
Red snapper	Swordfish	Haddock
Sardines	Whitefish	Halibut
Sea trout		Lobster
Snails		Lox
		Octopus
		Oysters

Frequent	Occasional	Seldom
		Pickled herring
		Sea bass
		Shrimp
		Striped bass
		Turtle
		Yellowtail

Dairy* (Blood Type AB)

Frequent	Occasional	Seldom
Cottage cheese	Cheddar cheese	American cheese
Farmer cheese	Colby cheese	Blue cheese
Feta cheese	Cream cheese	Brie cheese
Goat cheese	Edam cheese	Butter
Goat's milk	Gouda cheese	Camembert cheese
Kefir	Gruyère cheese	Ice cream
Mozzarella cheese (fresh)	Jarlsberg cheese	Milk (whole)
Ricotta cheese	Milk (cow's; skim or 2%)	Parmesan cheese
Sour cream (low-fat)	Monterey Jack cheese	Provolone cheese
Yogurt (organic, plain)	Muenster cheese	Sherbet
	Romano cheese	
	Soy cheese	
	Soy milk	
	String cheese	
	Swiss cheese	
	Tofu cream cheese	
	Whey	
	Yogurt (frozen)	

* *Whenever possible, select cheese made from organic raw milk. The enzymes present encourage efficient metabolism and have the least likelihood of affecting mucous membranes and sinuses.*

Oils (Blood Type AB)

Frequent	Occasional	Seldom
Extra virgin olive oil	Canola oil	Avocado
Grapeseed oil	Cod liver oil	Corn oil
	Flaxseed oil*	Cottonseed oil
	Peanut oil	Safflower oil
		Sesame oil
		Sunflower oil

Do not cook with this oil.

Nuts and Seeds (Blood Type AB)

Frequent	Occasional	Seldom
Peanut butter (organic)	Almond butter (raw)	Hazelnuts
Peanuts (organic)	Almonds (raw)	Poppy seeds
Walnuts	Brazil nuts	Pumpkin seeds
	Cashews	Sesame butter (raw)
	Litchi nuts	Sesame seeds (raw)
	Macadamia nuts	Sunflower butter
	Pignoli nuts	Sunflower seeds
	Pistachios	(raw)

Beans (Blood Type AB)

Frequent	Occasional	Seldom
Green lentils	Broad beans	Adzuki beans
Navy beans	Cannellini beans	Black beans
Pinto beans	Great northern beans	Black-eyed peas
Red beans	Red lentils	Chickpeas
Soy beans	Tamarind beans	(garbanzos)
Tempeh	White beans	Fava beans
Tofu		Kidney beans
		Lima beans

Grains (Blood Type AB)

Frequent	Occasional	Seldom
Ezekiel bread	Amaranth	Artichoke pasta
Millet	Bagels	Buckwheat
Oat bran	Barley	Corn products
Oat flour	Bulgur	Kamut
Oatmeal	Couscous	Kasha
Rice	Cream of rice	Soba noodles
Rice bran	Cream of Wheat	
Rice crackers (not rice cakes)	Durum flour	
Rice flour	Ezekiel bagels*	
Rye bread	Grape-Nuts	
Rye crackers	Muesli	
Rye flour	Quinoa	
Spelt	Semolina pasta	
Sprouted wheat bread	Seven-grain or multi-grain products	
	Shredded Wheat	
	Spinach pasta	
	Wheat bran	
	Wheat germ	

Ezekiel brand bagels have less fiber than Ezekiel bread. Hypoglycemics and diabetics may do better with Ezekiel bread, which is also better for weight loss.

Starchy Vegetables (Blood Type AB)

Frequent	Occasional	Seldom
Beets	Cooked carrots	Artichokes (all types)
Parsnips	Potatoes (red and white)	Corn
Sweet potatoes	Pumpkin	Lima beans
Yams		

Low-Starch Vegetables (Blood Type AB)

Frequent	Occasional	Seldom
Alfalfa sprouts	Arugula	Mushrooms (shiitake)
Beet greens	Asparagus	Olives (black)
Broccoli	Brussels sprouts	Peppers (all types)
Broccoli rabe	Cabbage (all types)	Radishes
Cauliflower	Coriander	Sprouts (mung, radish)
Celery	Daikon	
Collard greens	Endive	
Cucumber	Escarole	
Dandelion	Fennel	
Eggplant	Ferns	
Garlic	Ginger	
Kale	Horseradish	
Mustard greens	Kohlrabi	
Parsley	Leek	
	Lettuce (all types)	
	Mushrooms (Portobello, white, wild)	
	Okra	
	Olives (green, Greek, Spanish)	
	Onions (all types)	
	Radicchio	
	Rutabaga	
	Scallions	
	Seaweed	
	Snow peas	
	Spinach	
	Swiss chard	
	Tomato	
	Turnips	
	Water chestnuts	
	Watercress	
	Zucchini	

Fresh Fruits and Juices* (Blood Type AB)

Frequent	Occasional	Seldom
Cabbage juice	Apple juice	Bananas
Carrot juice	Apples	Guavas
Celery juice	Apricot juice	Mangoes
Cherries	Apricots	Oranges
Cherry juice	Blackberries	Persimmons
Cranberries	Blueberries	Pomegranates
Cranberry juice	Boysenberries	Prickly pears
Figs (all types)	Currants, all types	Rhubarb
Gooseberries	Dates	Star fruit
Grapefruit	Elderberries	
Grapefruit juice	Kumquats	
Grape juice	Limes	
Grapes (all types)	Melon (all types)	
Kiwis	Nectarines	
Lemons	Peaches	
Loganberries	Pears	
Papaya	Prune juice	
Papaya juice	Prunes	
(unsweetened)	Raisins	
Pineapple	Raspberries	
Pineapple juice	Strawberries	
Plums (all types)	Tangerines	

** Juices, in general, are not recommended for weight loss unless freshly squeezed.
Only organic fresh fruit and unsweetened juices are recommended.*

Beverages (Blood Type AB)

Frequent	Occasional	Seldom
Alfalfa tea	Beer*	Black tea (all types)
Burdock tea	Dandelion tea	Corn silk tea
Chamomile tea	Dong quai tea	Fenugreek tea
Coffee (all types)	Goldenseal tea	Lindon tea
Echinacea tea	Parsley tea	Liquor (all types)*

(continued)

Frequent	Occasional	Seldom
Ginger tea	Peppermint tea	Red clover tea
Ginseng tea	Raspberry leaf tea	Rhubarb tea
Green tea	St. John's wort tea	Senna tea
Hawthorn tea	Slippery elm tea	Sodas (all types)
Licorice root tea	Valerian tea	
Rose hips tea	Vervain tea	
Strawberry leaf tea	Wine (all types)*	
	Yellow dock tea	

* If you do not drink alcohol, please do not take this recommendation as an encouragement to start drinking.

One Week of Sample Weight-Loss Menus for Blood Type AB

Day 1

Breakfast: Fresh pineapple, kiwis, and strawberries
Lunch: Hard-boiled eggs in a spinach salad
Dinner: Turkey burgers with curried greens

Day 2

Breakfast: Cantaloupe
Lunch: Caesar Salad* with grilled turkey
Dinner: Red snapper with broccoli and a tossed salad

Day 3

Breakfast: Watermelon
Lunch: Sardines in a large green salad
Dinner: 1 cup pinto beans with 1/2 cup brown rice and sautéed greens

Food Combining Chart: Blood Type AB

Proteins*

Navy beans	Venison	Rabbit
Pinto beans	Lamb	Organic 1% milk
Lentils	Turkey	Organic eggs
Split peas	Fish	White cheese
Soy beans	Scallops	Yogurt
Tofu	Buffalo	*Eat only one protein food at a meal.

POOR TO COMBINE

GOOD TO COMBINE

Starches

Brown rice	Acorn squash	Millet
Potatoes	Yams	Frozen peas
Cooked carrots	Pumpkin	Spelt
Beets	Butternut squash	Ezekiel bread
Chestnuts	Parsnips	

GOOD TO COMBINE

Green and Low-Starch Vegetables

Cabbage	Onions	Watercress	Sugar snap peas	Cauliflower
Broccoli	Spinach	Bok choy	Garlic	Snow peas
Brussels sprouts	Zucchini	Asparagus	Escarole	Collard greens
Eggplant	Fresh peas	String beans	Lettuce	Kale
Alfalfa sprouts	Turnips			

Arugula	Tomatoes
Fennel	Mushrooms
Cucumber	Endive
Kohlrabi	Radicchio
	Raw carrots

Fats and Oils (combine with protein or starch)

Walnuts	Grapeseed oil	Soy margarine*
Olive oil	Peanuts (in the shell)	Mayonnaise

Raw almond butter
Organic peanut butter

*Use unhydrogenated margarine.

Acid Fruits

Lemons
Grapefruit
Limes
Strawberries

Kiwis
Pineapple
Kumquats
Cranberries

POOR TO COMBINE

Sub-Acid Fruits

Plums	Apricots
Mangoes	Apples
Pears	Nectarines
Berries	Cherries
Peaches	Green grapes

POOR TO COMBINE

Sweet Fruits

Fresh figs	Papaya
Fresh dates	Sapote
Grapes (purple, black)	Dried figs
	Prunes

Melons (poor to combine / eat alone)

Crenshaw	Honeydew	Cantaloupe	Watermelon

Day 4

Breakfast: Fresh figs
Lunch: Large bowl Creamy Lentil Soup* with 1 slice Ezekiel toast
Dinner: Turkey burger with sautéed spinach and a mixed green salad

Day 5

Breakfast: Grapefruit and strawberries
Lunch: Turkey burger with sautéed veggies
Dinner: Baked cod with Swiss chard and turnips

Day 6

Breakfast: Grapes
Lunch: Mock Greek Salad*
Dinner: Tofu spinach lasagna

Day 7

Breakfast: Pears and plums
Lunch: Low-fat organic cottage cheese with a spinach salad
Dinner: Lamb chops with sautéed escarole and Marinated Cold
    Asparagus*

Recipe is included in recipe section.

Sample Maintenance Menus for Blood Type AB

Day 1

Breakfast: Organic low-fat yogurt with berries
Lunch: Lentil soup with 1 slice Ezekiel bread and a green salad
Dinner: Baked red snapper in a curry sauce with basmati rice and grilled
    vegetables

Day 2

Breakfast: $^3/_4$ cup wheat-free granola with organic 1% milk
Lunch: Turkey breast topping a Caesar Salad*
Dinner: Lamb chops with sautéed vegetables and roasted yams

Day 3

Breakfast: Ezekiel bagel with organic cream cheese
Lunch: Pinto bean salad with marinated string beans
Dinner: Spelt spaghetti and vegetable ragout

Day 4

Breakfast: Rice flour pancakes with pure maple syrup or fruit juice-sweetened jam
Lunch: Turkey burger or meat loaf and coleslaw
Dinner: Make your own pizza with a tossed salad

Day 5

Breakfast: 1 slice Ezekiel toast with 2 turkey breakfast sausages
Lunch: Sardines on 1 slice Ezekiel bread and a spinach salad
Dinner: Turkey cutlets cut in strips, sautéed with onions and vegetables

Day 6

Breakfast: Yogurt smoothie with vanilla yogurt and frozen berries
Lunch: Egg salad on an Ezekiel bagel and coleslaw
Dinner: Lentil and rice pilaf with sautéed greens

Day 7

Breakfast: Oatmeal cooked in soy milk or 1% milk
Lunch: Fresh mozzarella cheese on Ezekiel bread with marinated eggplant and a slice of tomato
Dinner: Scallops sautéed in olive oil, garlic, and white wine with Chinese vegetables and $^1/_2$ cup rice noodles with peanut sauce

Recipe is included in recipe section.

Meals for the Whole Family

Here is a wide variety of delicious meals for families whose members have different blood types. The meals can be used either for lunch or dinner. Cooked greens can be added to or substituted for the mesclun salad greens.

The following recipes are compatible with all blood types except the following:

Blood type O should avoid yogurt and dairy products.

Blood type B should avoid tofu and soy products.

Blood type A should avoid all red meat.

Blood types AB and B should avoid chicken and limit salmon.

In addition, be sure to consult the food combining chart and food lists for your specific blood type to make sure this meal is compatible for you. Use organic ingredients whenever possible. Recipes for nearly all dishes are included in the next chapter.

The following recipes are compatible for all blood types except when specified:

- Mesclun or organic greens/sprouts
  - with Turkey and Curry or Tamari Mayonnaise*
  - with Delectable Dilled Egg or Tuna Salad*
  - with Basic Turkey Salad* with tarragon
  - with canned tuna, salmon, or sardines and Lemon-Garlic-Oregano Dressing*
- Caesar Salad*, either plain or with cold sliced turkey or chicken
- Spinach, Mushroom, and Feta Cheese Salad with Lemon-Garlic-Oregano Dressing*
- Mock Greek Salad*
- Arugula and Portobello Mushroom Salad*
- Boston Lettuce and Belgian Endive Salad with avocado*
- Cucumber and Feta Salad*
- Codfish Salad*
- Cold Tofu Salad*
- Asparagus Soup with a Boston Lettuce and Belgian Endive Salad*

- Cold Cucumber and Yogurt Soup with mesclun greens and Curry Vinaigrette*
- Creamy Lentil Soup with mesclun greens and Low-Cal Yogurt Dressing*
- Fantastic French Onion Soup with a Boston Lettuce and Belgian Endive Salad*
- Grandma's Vegetable Chicken Soup*
- Indian-Spiced Spinach Soup with mesclun greens and Curry Vinaigrette*
- Mediterranean Vegetable Soup with mesclun greens and Lemon-Garlic-Oregano Dressing*
- Meme's Miso Soup with Cold Oriental Bean Sprouts*
- Simply Split Pea Soup with Low-Cal Yogurt Dressing*
- Organic brown rice with stir-fried or steamed vegetables of your choice seasoned with tamari
- Lentils with Spinach plus a salad of your choice with Annie's Naturals Goddess Dressing*
- Stir-Fried Toasted Rice*
- Omelet with fresh herbs or lightly sautéed, grated veggies of your choice
- All natural turkey hot dogs and Fennel Broccoli Slaw*
- Cooked Oriental Tofu and Broccoli or String Beans Oriental*
- Adele's Asian Adventure with Fish and Veggies*
- Basic Broiled Fish with a Caesar or Arugula and Portobello Mushroom Salad*
- Broiled Fish with a Zip and Spinach with Yogurt*
- Broiled Fish Kabobs and String Beans with Shallots*
- Basic Poached Fish with Aioli Sauce and steamed vegetables of your choice*
- Baked Tandoori Fish with Cucumber and Yogurt Raita*
- Biovanna's Sautéed Tuna with Broccoli Rabe, Italian-Style or Garlic Escarole*
- Seared tuna with Sautéed Fennel*
- Turkey or Chicken Cutlets with Lemon* and broccoli with garlic

- Garlic- and Basil-Infused Turkey Breast with Baked Zucchini or Roasted Fennel*
- Grilled Turkey Tenderloins with Curry Mayonnaise and Cucumber and Yogurt Raita plus Zucchini with Fresh Herbs*
- Basic Broiled Chicken (or turkey) with a Caesar Salad and Slightly Sautéed Spinach with Garlic*
- Marinated Broiled Chicken (or turkey) with String Beans with Shallots*
- Bean Dip and Crudités*
- Cannellini Minestrone*
- Broiled Chicken (or turkey) with Mustard and an Arugula and Portobello Mushroom Salad*
- Roasted Chicken (or turkey) with Herbs with Asparagus in Tarragon Sauce or String Beans with Lemon*
- Sautéed Chicken with Fresh Rosemary and Zucchini with Fresh Herbs*
- Teriyaki Chicken and Broccoli or String Beans Oriental*
- Herb-Crusted Roast Leg of Lamb and Cauliflower with Indian Spices plus Spiced Leeks*
- Broiled Boneless Butterflied Leg of Lamb and Roasted Fennel and/or Baked Zucchini*
- Broiled Mustard London Broil or Steak with Spiced Leeks and an Arugula and Portobello Mushroom Salad*
- Refried Beans*, brown rice, and a green salad
- Mung or Adzuki Bean Stew*

Recipe is included in recipe section.

CHAPTER FOUR

Recipes

Salads and Salad Dressings

Salads

Basic Chicken or Turkey Salad

2 cups cooked chicken or turkey, diced

2 tablespoons Basic Mayonnaise (recipe on page 73)
   or store bought mayonnaise

$^1/_2$ cup celery, finely chopped

1 tablespoon minced Bermuda onion or shallot

Mix together all of the ingredients and serve with a mesclun green salad and sprouts and a dressing of your choice. Other versions of this salad can be prepared by using different flavors of mayonnaise, such as curry, tarragon, or tamari.

Serves 2.

Delectable Dilled Egg or Tuna Salad

2 hard-boiled eggs or 1 can of solid white tuna, drained

$^1/_2$ tablespoon Basic Mayonnaise (recipe on page 73)
   or store bought mayonnaise

$^1/_2$ teaspoon minced fresh dill or $^1/_4$ teaspoon dry dill

$^1/_4$ cup celery, finely chopped

2 teaspoons minced Bermuda onion

Sea salt and pepper to taste

Chop the hard-boiled eggs or crumble the drained tuna and add all of the other ingredients. Serve on a bed of organic mesclun greens with sprouts and a dressing of your choice.

Variation: If you prefer, Curry Mayonnaise (recipe on page 74) can be added to the chopped hard-boiled eggs instead of the minced dill.

Serves 1.

Mock Greek Salad

1 cup organic mesclun greens

$^1/_2$ cup fresh feta cheese

Small handful clover sprouts

2 tablespoons Bermuda onion, thinly sliced

Lemon-Garlic-Oregano Dressing (recipe on page 74)

Prepare the salad greens and crumble the feta cheese on top. Cover with sprouts and onions. Drizzle dressing on salad to taste.

Variation: As an alternative to the feta cheese, crumble a can of solid white tuna on top of the salad. The tuna is especially delicious when combined with this dressing.

Serves 1.

Spinach, Mushroom, and Feta Cheese Salad

$^1/_2$ pound fresh spinach

12 button mushrooms, thinly sliced

Bermuda onion, sliced (as much as desired)

$^1/_2$ pound fresh feta cheese, crumbled

Lemon-Garlic-Oregano Dressing (recipe on page 74) to taste

Wash spinach thoroughly, break into bite-size pieces, and spin dry. Gently toss in the thinly sliced mushrooms and the Bermuda onion slices. Top with the feta cheese and slowly drizzle the dressing to taste.

Serves 1.

Caesar Salad

3 or 4 organic romaine lettuce hearts

Perfect Caesar Salad Dressing (recipe on page 75) to taste

$^1/_4$ cup freshly grated Romano cheese

Cut, wash, and spin dry bite-size pieces of romaine lettuce. Slowly add dressing to the lettuce and gently toss. Add the grated Romano cheese and blend fully. Serve immediately. This recipe makes approximately four side salads or two main course salads.

Variation: To make it a more substantial meal, add cold, sliced cooked chicken or turkey. Caesar Salad makes an excellent accompaniment to grilled or broiled fresh tuna steak or salmon fillet.

Serves 2 to 4.

Arugula and Portobello Mushroom Salad

1 large bunch of organic arugula

3 Portobello mushrooms, medium-sized

1 tablespoon grapeseed oil or extra virgin olive oil

Sea salt and freshly ground pepper to taste

2 tablespoons organic extra virgin olive oil

1 teaspoon rice vinegar (optional)

Wash and spin dry the arugula and chill until ready to use, to retain crispness. Cut the Portobello mushrooms into $1/4$-inch slices and sauté in the oil in a large enough pan to fit all of the slices in a single layer. The mushrooms should turn a golden-brown color on both sides. Remove the mushrooms from the heat and let cool. Lightly season with sea salt and pepper. To make the dressing, blend the olive oil, rice vinegar, sea salt, and pepper in a tightly sealed container. Place the arugula on a plate and arrange the mushrooms on top. Slowly drizzle the dressing on the salad. This salad is an especially good combination with organic sliced lamb or steak. It is also a great side salad with broiled or grilled salmon.

Extra dressing should be refrigerated.

Serves 2.

Boston Lettuce and Belgian Endive Salad

2 heads Boston lettuce

3 small heads Belgian endive

Mustard vinaigrette (recipe on page 76) to taste

Break lettuce into bite-size pieces, wash, and spin dry. Discard the central core of the endive. Cut the endive into horizontal thin slices about $1/2$ inch thick. Mix together the lettuce and endive. Slowly drizzle the dressing onto the salad to taste, and gently toss. This light salad is an excellent accompaniment to grilled or broiled fresh fish or organic red meat.

Serves 1.

Cucumber and Feta Cheese Salad

5 or 6 Kirby cucumbers

1 small Bermuda onion, thinly sliced

Sea salt and freshly ground pepper to taste

3 tablespoons each fresh mint, parsley, and chives, chopped

$^1/_2$ pound fresh feta cheese, crumbled

2 tablespoons organic extra virgin olive oil

1 tablespoon rice wine vinegar

Peel and thinly slice the cucumbers. Place the slices in a container and chill for at least 30 minutes. Peel and thinly slice the onion. Place the onion slices in a container, cover with cold water, and chill for 30 minutes. When you are ready to prepare the salad, drain and dry the onion slices and layer them with the cucumber on a large platter. Season with sea salt, freshly ground pepper, and the chopped fresh herbs. Scatter the cheese on top. Whisk the olive oil and vinegar together and drizzle it evenly on the salad.

Serves 4.

Codfish Salad

$2^1/_2$ pounds cod fillets

1 bunch cilantro, chopped

3 tablespoons fresh mint, chopped

2 tablespoons fresh chives, chopped

3 medium cloves garlic, minced

Sea salt and freshly ground pepper to taste

$^1/_4$ teaspoon ground cumin

Juice of 2 large lemons

2 tablespoons organic extra virgin olive oil

1 head Boston lettuce

Preheat oven to 375°F. Rinse and dry the fillets and bake them for approximately 8 minutes or until they are opaque and flake easily with a fork. Remove from the oven and let cool. Place the cod in a large bowl. In a separate dish, blend together the remaining ingredients, excluding the Boston lettuce. Measure out half of the herb/spice mixture and toss with the cod. Cover and chill. Separate the leaves of the Boston lettuce, wash, and dry. Place equal amounts of the lettuce leaves on four individual serving plates. Remove the fish mixture from the refrigerator and add the remaining herb/spice mixture. Season with additional sea salt and pepper if desired. Serve immediately.

Serves 4.

Cold Tofu Salad

1 pound firm organic tofu
4 cups fresh bean sprouts or 1 3.5-ounce package of snow pea shoots
Annie's Naturals Shiitake and Sesame Vinaigrette
$^1/_4$ cup scallion green tops, thinly sliced for garnish

Drain tofu and pat dry. Cut tofu into 1-inch cubes. Place bean sprouts in a container with the tofu. Slowly drizzle dressing over the mixture. Cover and shake gently to evenly coat the ingredients. Chill until ready to serve. The tofu will absorb the flavor of the dressing and provide a richer taste. When serving, garnish with the sliced scallion tops. If you are lucky enough to find snow pea shoots, prepare the tofu as suggested but combine with the shoots and dressing when you are ready to serve the salad. Then garnish with the scallions.

Serves 3.

Salad Dressings

Basic Mayonnaise

This mayonnaise recipe is quick and easy to make and is much healthier than a supermarket brand. If time is short, use canola mayonnaise from the health-food store.

1 organic egg yolk

Pinch of sea salt

$^1/_2$ teaspoon Dijon or stone-ground mustard

$^2/_3$ cup organic extra virgin olive oil or grapeseed oil

2 teaspoons freshly squeezed lemon juice

Put egg yolk, salt, and mustard in a blender and process for about 20 seconds. While continuing to blend, slowly add the olive or grapeseed oil, and the mixture will thicken. Add the lemon juice. Store in refrigerator.

Grapeseed Oil

Grapeseed oil is a by-product of wine production. It has been a favorite among European chefs because of its quality. The oil has the highest smoking point when compared to other oils, which makes it ideal for sautéing and baking. Thus, it can take very high heat without burning. Recent studies have shown that grapeseed oil may also be effective in helping to lower cholesterol levels in individuals at cardiac risk.[16] Grapeseed oil is one of the very few natural foods to raise HDL cholesterol. Research confirms that in each percent increase in HDL, there will be a 3 to 4 percent decrease in cardiac disease.[17] Grapeseed oil is an excellent source of vitamin E and essential fatty acids. Recipes calling for olive oil may substitute grapeseed oil, which is lighter in taste and consistency than olive oil.

Curry Mayonnaise

1 tablespoon curry powder

$^1/_4$ teaspoon ground cumin

$^1/_4$ teaspoon ground coriander

$^1/_4$ teaspoon turmeric

$^1/_4$ teaspoon ground cinnamon

Mix all the spices together and put in a small shaker jar. Sprinkle over and mix into mayonnaise to taste. The spice mixture can be stored and used for preparing future curry mayonnaise.

Variations: For Tarragon Mayonnaise, add 1 or 2 tablespoons finely minced fresh tarragon or $^1/_2$ teaspoon dried tarragon to 1 cup mayonnaise.

For Tamari Mayonnaise, add 2 or 3 teaspoons tamari to 1 cup mayonnaise.

Lemon-Garlic-Oregano Dressing

This is a favorite dressing of friends and family. It is so simple to make and is an outstanding addition to the Spinach, Mushroom, and Feta Cheese Salad (see page 69) or a simple green salad with feta cheese.

Juice of 1 large lemon

1 medium clove garlic, pressed

$^1/_2$ teaspoon dried oregano

$^1/_3$ cup organic extra virgin olive oil or grapeseed oil

$^1/_2$ teaspoon sea salt

Freshly ground pepper to taste

Whisk together all of the ingredients and blend thoroughly. Store in a container and shake well before adding it to a salad. Keep refrigerated.

Low-Cal Yogurt Dressing

1 tablespoon lemon juice, freshly squeezed

1 teaspoon honey

1 teaspoon Dijon or stone-ground mustard

2 cloves garlic, pressed

2/3 cup organic plain low-fat yogurt

Sea salt and freshly ground pepper to taste

Whisk together the lemon juice and honey until fully blended. Add remaining ingredients and combine thoroughly. Chill for several hours before using.

Perfect Caesar Salad Dressing

Juice of 1 large lemon

1/2 tube of anchovy paste

1 large clove garlic, pressed

1 tablespoon Worchestershire sauce

1/2 cup organic extra virgin olive oil or grapeseed oil

Whisk together all of the ingredients and blend them thoroughly. Store in a container and shake well before adding to the salad, a little at a time to taste. This recipe makes enough dressing for approximately two packages of organic romaine lettuce hearts. If refrigerated, this dressing can be used for up to 3 days.

Mustard Vinaigrette

2 tablespoons Dijon or stone-ground mustard

1 tablespoon raw cold-pressed apple cider vinegar

$^1/_4$ teaspoon salt

Freshly ground pepper to taste

$^1/_4$ cup organic extra virgin olive oil or grapeseed oil

2 tablespoons fresh minced tarragon or $^1/_2$ teaspoon dried tarragon

Whisk together the mustard, vinegar, salt, and pepper, and blend well. Slowly add the olive or grapeseed oil, a little at a time until the dressing has a thickened texture. Add the tarragon and blend thoroughly. This dressing is superb on a Boston Lettuce and Belgian Endive Salad (see page 70). Remember: When adding a dressing to a salad, always add a little at a time. Too much dressing can overpower the flavor and oversaturate the greens.

Curry Vinaigrette

1 tablespoon curry

$^1/_4$ teaspoon ground cumin

$^1/_4$ teaspoon ground coriander

$^1/_2$ teaspoon turmeric

$^1/_2$ teaspoon ground cinnamon

1 clove garlic, pressed

$^1/_2$ teaspoon fresh ginger, peeled and grated

$1^1/_2$ tablespoons lemon juice

$^1/_4$ teaspoon sea salt

6 tablespoons organic extra virgin olive oil or grapeseed oil

Blend together the curry, cumin, coriander, turmeric, and cinnamon. Measure 2 teaspoons of the spice mixture and mix with the garlic, ginger, lemon juice, and sea salt. Whisk in the olive oil. Store the remaining spice mixture to mix with mayonnaise or a future dressing.

Soups

Asparagus Soup

1 pound thin asparagus, tough ends removed

3 tablespoons organic butter or organic extra virgin olive oil

3 medium leeks, white parts only, sliced

$1/2$ teaspoon sea salt or more if desired

1 tablespoon parsley, chopped

6 cups vegetable broth

Freshly ground pepper to taste

$1/2$ teaspoon grated lemon peel

Chop the asparagus into 1-inch pieces. Melt the butter or heat the oil in a stock pot, and add the leeks. Cook them over medium-high heat for approximately 3 minutes, stirring occasionally. Add the asparagus, salt, and parsley. Pour in the vegetable broth and bring to a boil. Simmer until the asparagus is tender, about 6 minutes. Let cool. Then purée the soup in a blender. Return the soup to the stove, and season with sea salt and freshly ground pepper to taste. Stir in the grated lemon peel and serve.

Serves 4.

Cold Cucumber and Yogurt Soup

4 large cucumbers

2 cups canned or cartons of chicken broth

1 small clove garlic

2 tablespoons minced Bermuda onion

2 cups organic plain low-fat yogurt

1 tablespoon brown rice or raw organic apple cider vinegar

Sea salt and freshly ground pepper to taste

Peel the cucumbers. Cut them in half lengthwise and then cut them in half again. Remove the seeds and cut the remaining cucumber into large chunks. Place half of the cucumber and broth plus all of the garlic and onion into a blender. Blend until puréed. Pour mixture into a large bowl. Blend the remaining cucumber and broth and add to the mixture in the bowl. Add the yogurt, vinegar, salt, and pepper and whisk all ingredients until smooth. Chill for at least 4 hours. For best results, chill overnight.

Serves 6.

Creamy Lentil Soup

1 tablespoon organic extra virgin olive oil

1 large onion, chopped

2 medium-sized cloves garlic, pressed

2 celery stalks, chopped

2 cups lentils, rinsed

8 cups water, filtered if possible

1 bay leaf

Sea salt and freshly ground pepper to taste

1 1/2 teaspoons ground cumin

Heat the oil in a stock pot and sauté onion, garlic, and celery until wilted. Add the lentils, water, and bay leaf. Bring to a boil, cover, and simmer until lentils are tender, about 45 minutes. Add the salt, pepper, and cumin. Simmer for an additional 10 minutes. Remove the bay leaf and let the soup cool before puréeing in a blender. Reheat when ready to serve. For a thicker consistency, let the soup simmer uncovered a bit longer.

Serves 6.

Fantastic French Onion Soup

2 $1/2$ pounds onions, thinly sliced

2 tablespoons expeller-pressed grapeseed or olive oil

1 tablespoon organic butter or canola oil margarine (unhydrogenated)

$1/2$ teaspoon dry mustard

5 cups chicken broth*

5 cups beef broth*

$1/2$ teaspoon dried sage

1 bay leaf

$1/4$ cup dry white wine

Sauté the onions in the oil and butter for 30 minutes, over medium-low heat. Stir in the dry mustard and sauté for an additional 30 minutes. Occasionally, stir the onions to prevent sticking. Add the remaining ingredients and simmer for 45 minutes. This soup tastes even better when served a day or two later.

Serves 6.

* Chicken and beef broth are fine for all blood types.

Grandma's Vegetable Chicken Soup

1 large organic roasting chicken

8 cups water, filtered if possible

1 medium onion

1 tablespoon sea salt or as desired

$1/4$ teaspoon white pepper

2 parsnips

3 organic carrots

1 medium-sized turnip

4 stems organic celery

4 sprigs fresh parsley

8 sprigs fresh dill

Thoroughly wash chicken, neck, and gizzard. Place these in a large pot with the water, onion, salt, and pepper. Bring to a boil. Continually skim off the scum from the soup. Meanwhile, peel the parsnips, carrots, and turnip, and cut these veggies into bite-size pieces. Clean and cut the celery into bite-size pieces. Let chicken cook over medium-low heat for about 30 minutes before adding the veggies, parsley, and dill. Check broth to discern if additional sea salt needs to be added. Simmer for about 45 minutes or until chicken is easily pulled apart. Remove the chicken, neck, and gizzard from the pot along with the onion, dill, and parsley. Discard the neck, gizzard, onion, dill, and parsley. The cooked chicken can be used to make chicken salad. Let the soup remain in the refrigerator overnight. Before reheating the soup, remove all of the fat that has gathered at the top and discard.

Serves 6.

Indian-Spiced Spinach Soup

2 tablespoons organic butter

1 large Bermuda onion, sliced

3 large cloves garlic, minced

3 tablespoons brown rice or white basmati rice

$^1/_2$ teaspoon sea salt or more to taste

$^1/_2$ teaspoon ground cloves

$^1/_2$ teaspoon ground cumin

$^1/_8$ teaspoon ground nutmeg

7 cups vegetable broth

$1^1/_2$ pounds fresh spinach, stems removed, and washed

Grated peel and juice of 1 lemon

Freshly ground pepper to taste

In a large soup pot, melt butter and sauté onion slices, garlic, rice, and salt. Cook for about 5 minutes over medium-low heat. Add the cloves, cumin, and nutmeg. Cook, stirring occasionally, for an additional 5 minutes. Add $1^1/_2$ cups vegetable broth and simmer for 10 minutes. Add the spinach leaves to the pot until they wilt. Add the remaining broth. Bring to a boil and simmer 5 minutes. Cool the soup, then purée it in a blender. Return the soup to the pot and stir in the grated lemon peel. Add the lemon juice to taste and additional sea salt and freshly ground pepper, if desired.

Serves 4.

Mediterranean Vegetable Soup

2 tablespoons or less organic extra virgin olive oil

5 small leeks, white parts only, cut into $^{1}/_{2}$-inch slices

4 celery stalks, diced

1 tablespoon lemon juice, freshly squeezed

1 teaspoon sea salt or more if desired

6 cups water, filtered if possible

1 cup sweet green peas

1 cup romaine lettuce, shredded

1 small bunch fresh spinach, stems removed

Sea salt to taste

1 tablespoon fresh parsley, finely chopped

1 tablespoon fresh mint, finely chopped

Heat the olive oil in a large pot, add the leeks, celery, lemon juice, and salt. Cover the pot and simmer over medium-low heat for approximately 15 minutes. Be sure to stir occasionally to prevent the veggies from sticking. Add the water, peas, lettuce, and spinach. Simmer for an additional 10 minutes until wilted. When the soup has cooled, place it in a blender and purée. Add additional sea salt to taste, if desired. Stir in the parsley and mint, just before serving.

Serves 4.

Meme's Miso Soup

3 $1/3$ cups low-salt chicken stock or filtered water

4 tablespoons organic traditional red miso

$1/2$ cake soft organic tofu, cut into $1/2$-inch cubes

1 package enoki mushrooms

$1/4$ cup green scallion tops, thinly sliced

Heat the stock until almost boiling. Scoop out $1/2$ cup of the stock and blend with the miso. Slowly add the miso stock mixture to the rest of the stock. Blend well and add the tofu, mushrooms, and scallions. Serve immediately.

Serves 4.

Simply Split Pea Soup

2 cups organic green split peas

8 cups cold filtered water

1 medium yellow onion

1 clove garlic, sliced

2 bay leaves

2 teaspoons sea salt or to taste

White pepper to taste

3 medium organic carrots

4 stalks organic celery

$1/2$ cup dry white wine

Place the split peas, water, whole onion, garlic, bay leaves, sea salt, and white pepper in a large pot and cook over medium heat. Stir constantly to prevent sticking. Meanwhile, peel the carrots and cut them into $1/2$-inch rounds. Clean celery and cut into $1/2$-inch pieces. When the soup begins to boil, remove scum from the surface. Add the wine, carrots, and celery. Simmer and stir the soup over low heat for 1 hour or until the split peas are tender. Remove the whole onion and bay leaves and adjust the taste by adding additional sea salt and pepper if necessary. If the soup is too thick, water may be added to achieve a thinner consistency. This soup can also be puréed in a blender if desired.

Serves 4.

Vegetables

Marinated Cold Asparagus

1 pound asparagus, tough ends removed
$^1/_4$ cup Lemon-Garlic-Oregano Dressing (recipe on page 74) to taste
Sea salt and freshly ground pepper to taste

Steam or cook asparagus for 2 to 5 minutes, until slightly tender. Remove from heat and rinse under cool water. Drain and place in a sealed container and chill for about 1 hour. Pour dressing on the asparagus and continue to chill until ready to serve. Gently toss before serving to coat asparagus with dressing. Season with salt and pepper as desired. This is a delicious accompaniment to grilled fish or red meat.

Serves 4.

Asparagus in Tarragon Sauce

1 pound asparagus, tough ends removed
1 teaspoon organic extra virgin olive oil
Green ends of 3 scallions, sliced into $^1/_4$-inch pieces
1 tablespoon fresh tarragon, minced
Sea salt to taste
1 tablespoon lemon juice
2 tablespoons water

Steam or cook asparagus for 2 to 5 minutes, until slightly tender. Remove from heat and rinse under cool water. Drain and place on a serving dish. Heat the olive oil in a small pan, and sauté the scallions for 1 minute. Add the tarragon, sea salt, lemon juice, and water. Cook over medium heat for an additional minute. Drizzle evenly over the asparagus to cover. Serve immediately.

Serves 4 as a side dish.

Cold Oriental Bean Sprouts

$^1/_4$ cup Annie's Naturals Shiitake and Sesame Vinaigrette
1 pound bean sprouts

Drizzle dressing on the sprouts and toss well. Add additional dressing if necessary, but be sure not to oversaturate. Chill for 2 hours before serving. This is an excellent side accompaniment to Teriyaki Chicken (recipe on page 113) or salmon.

Serves 3 to 4 as a side dish.

Broccoli or String Beans Oriental

4 cups organic fresh broccoli florets or fresh string beans, trimmed
1 tablespoon expeller-pressed grapeseed or olive oil
1 teaspoon fresh garlic, minced
1 teaspoon fresh ginger, minced
1 tablespoon tamari wheat-free soy sauce

Steam or cook broccoli or string beans so that they remain slightly crisp. Rinse under cold water and drain. In a nonstick fry pan, heat oil and add garlic and ginger, stirring constantly. Do not allow to brown. Add the broccoli or string beans and coat them with the garlic and ginger. Quickly stir-fry. Sprinkle tamari over the vegetables and blend. Serve immediately. This is a delicious side dish with salmon, chicken, or lamb.

Variation: You could also serve these vegetables with tofu. Just add cubed firm tofu when sautéing the ginger and garlic. These vegetables can also be served over a bed of brown rice.

Serves 2 to 4.

Broccoli Rabe, Italian Style

1 tablespoon organic extra virgin olive oil

3 teaspoons garlic, finely chopped

1 pound broccoli rabe, rinsed and cut into 3-inch pieces

$1/4$ cup dry white wine or chicken broth

Sea salt and freshly ground pepper to taste

Heat olive oil in a 12-inch nonstick skillet. Remove from heat and stir in the garlic for 30 seconds. Toss the broccoli rabe and cook over medium heat for about 1 minute. Add the wine or broth and simmer uncovered for about 5 minutes. Salt and pepper to taste, cover, and simmer until the broccoli is tender. To serve, spoon the broccoli rabe and its liquid in a bowl as a vegetable meal, onto a bed of brown rice as a starch meal, or with fish as a protein meal.

Serves 1 to 3.

Cauliflower with Indian Spices

1 medium cauliflower

1 tablespoon grapeseed oil

1 tablespoon fresh ginger, finely minced

$1^1/2$ teaspoons ground cumin

$1/2$ teaspoon turmeric

$1/4$ cup and 2 tablespoons filtered water

Sea salt and freshly ground pepper to taste

Cut cauliflower into bite-size florets, wash, and drain. Steam the cauliflower or boil for 3 minutes. Drain. Heat the oil in a large pan over low heat. Sauté the ginger over medium heat for about 30 seconds. Reduce the heat to low and blend the cumin and turmeric with the ginger. Add the cauliflower florets, making sure to coat them evenly with the spice mixture. Blend in 2 tablespoons of water, salt, and pepper and stir. When the water evaporates, add the remaining water, cover tightly, and simmer until cauliflower is tender. Add additional salt and pepper to taste, if desired. This dish is excellent when served with lamb or basmati rice.

Serves 2 to 4.

Cucumber and Yogurt Raita

3 medium cucumbers

$^1/_2$ teaspoon garlic, finely chopped

1 $^1/_2$ cups organic plain low-fat yogurt

1 teaspoon grapeseed oil

$^1/_2$ teaspoon ground cumin

Sea salt to taste

Pinch of white pepper

Cut the cucumbers into quarters lengthwise and remove the seeds. Finely grate the cucumbers and place into a paper towel–lined colander to drain excess liquid. In a bowl, blend together the cucumber, garlic, yogurt, oil, and cumin. Add the sea salt and adjust to taste. Add the pepper. Chill for at least 1 hour before serving.

Serves 3 to 4.

Garlic Escarole

2 heads of escarole, cored and washed

6 cloves garlic

2 tablespoons organic extra virgin olive oil

Sea salt and freshly ground pepper to taste

Place the escarole leaves in a large bowl that is filled with very cold water. Swish leaves and drain to remove any dirt. Fill three-quarters of a large pot with salted filtered water and bring to a boil. Add the escarole and make sure to submerge all the leaves. Simmer for 5 minutes and drain. Squeeze out any excess water. Cut the garlic into thin slivers. Dry out the large pot and heat the olive oil over a medium-high heat. Add the garlic and sauté until it is about to brown. Add the escarole. Add salt and pepper to taste. Garlic Escarole is an excellent side dish when served with grilled Turkey or Chicken Cutlets with Lemon (recipe on page 107).

Serves 1 to 4.

Fennel Broccoli Slaw

1 medium fennel bulb

2 medium organic carrots, peeled

6 large broccoli stems, peeled

Brianna's Homestyle Poppy Seed Dressing to taste

Sea salt to taste

Cut the fennel in half from top to bottom. Remove the core. Julienne or grate the fennel, carrots, and broccoli stems by hand or with a food processor. Blend together the grated fennel and carrot mixture with the dressing. Salt to taste. This is a delicious salad to serve with grilled or broiled organic chicken.

Serves 2.

Roasted Fennel

3 medium fennel bulbs
1 cup filtered water
1 tablespoon organic sweet butter
$^1/_4$ teaspoon ground nutmeg
Sea salt and freshly ground pepper to taste
Romano cheese, finely grated, to taste

Preheat oven to 375°F. Cut off the top of the fennel so that only the bulb remains. Remove any bruised outer leaves. Cut the bulbs in half cross-wise. Boil salted filtered water in a pot large enough to fit the fennel. Simmer for 10 minutes. Drain. Melt the butter and brush the bottom of a baking dish. Place the fennel in the dish and brush the pieces with the remaining butter. Sprinkle each piece evenly with the nutmeg, salt, pepper, and finally the Romano cheese. Bake until golden brown. This vegetable dish is superb when served with sliced Garlic- and Basil-Infused Turkey Breast (recipe on page 107).

Serves 4 to 6.

Spiced Leeks

4 medium leeks
$1^1/_2$ cups salted water
1 tablespoon organic sweet butter
Pinch of ground nutmeg
Sea salt and freshly ground pepper to taste

Cut off the bottom roots and green tops of the leeks. Cut leeks in half lengthwise. Wash well and drain. Boil leeks in a covered pan with salted filtered water until they are tender. Drain thoroughly in a colander. Dry pan and melt butter, making sure not to brown. Add the leeks. Sprinkle with nutmeg, salt, and pepper. Cook for 1 minute over medium-high heat and blend in spices. Leeks enhance the flavor of salmon, tuna, lamb, beef, and chicken dishes.

Serves 3 to 4.

String Beans with Shallots or Lemon

1 pound fresh organic string beans

1 tablespoon organic sweet butter

2 tablespoons shallots, minced, or juice of $^1/_2$ lemon

Sea salt and freshly ground pepper to taste

Snap the ends off the string beans. Wash and drain. Steam or blanch the beans in boiling water until they are tender or slightly crunchy. Rinse under cool water and drain. Make sure to dry out the same pan that you used to cook the string beans and then melt the butter. Add the shallots and sauté them for 1 minute over medium heat. Toss in the string beans and cook for an additional minute to coat them with the butter and shallots. Salt and pepper to taste. Serve immediately. This vegetable dish particularly complements grilled fresh tuna, chicken, or turkey dishes.

Variation: Alternatively, flavor the string beans with the juice of $^1/_2$ lemon instead of the shallots. Or use both!

Serves 4.

Slightly Sautéed Spinach with Garlic

1 tablespoon expeller-pressed grapeseed oil

2 or 3 cloves garlic, thinly sliced

1 pound fresh organic spinach, stemmed and washed

Sea salt and freshly ground pepper to taste

Heat the oil over medium-high heat. Add the garlic and sauté until almost brownish in color. Add the spinach and toss gently until wilted. Serve immediately with grilled fish or chicken.

Serves 2 to 4.

Spinach with Yogurt

1 pound fresh organic spinach, stemmed and washed

$1/2$ cup plain low-fat organic yogurt

Juice of 1 lemon

1 clove garlic, pressed

Sea salt and freshly ground pepper to taste

Wilt the spinach in the water clinging to its leaves in a nonstick pan over medium-high heat. Drain and press out the liquid. Place on a chopping board and chop fine. Mix in the yogurt, lemon juice, and garlic. Season to taste with sea salt and freshly ground pepper. Chill for at least 1 hour before serving. This refreshing dish can be eaten as a vegetable meal or combines nicely with lamb.

Serves 2 to 4.

Baked Zucchini

2 medium zucchini

$1/2$ tablespoon organic sweet butter, melted

Sea salt and freshly ground pepper to taste

$1/4$ teaspoon garlic powder

$1/4$ teaspoon sweet paprika

1 tablespoon Romano cheese

Preheat oven to 375°F. Cut the zucchini in half lengthwise. Place them in a baking dish large enough to hold the pieces so that they can lie flat in the dish. Brush the melted butter across the entire surface of each zucchini half. Sprinkle evenly with the salt, pepper, garlic powder, and paprika. Sprinkle each piece with approximately $1/2$ tablespoon of Romano cheese, being careful to spread evenly. Bake for 45 minutes or until the surface of the zucchini appears to be golden brown. Serve with swordfish, chicken, turkey, beef, or lamb.

Serves 2 to 4.

Zucchini with Fresh Herbs

1 pound medium zucchini

1 tablespoon organic extra virgin olive oil

Sea salt and freshly ground pepper to taste

1 tablespoon organic butter

1 $^{1}/_{2}$ teaspoons garlic, minced

1 tablespoon each fresh parsley, chives, dill, tarragon,
    and basil, chopped

Wash and dry the zucchini, discarding the ends. Cut them into $^{1}/_{8}$-inch slices. Heat the olive oil in a skillet and when hot add the zucchini slices. Sauté over high heat for about 5 minutes, carefully turning the pieces. Add salt and pepper. Drain in a strainer. Use the same skillet to melt the butter. Return the zucchini to the skillet and evenly spread the garlic and herbs over the zucchini. Toss and serve immediately. This delicate vegetable dish is delicious when combined with a bowl of brown rice or fish.

Serves 1 to 4.

Steamed Greens

A variety of greens, including beet greens, collards, kale, and Swiss chard, is readily available in supermarkets. These leaves can be steamed and wilted until they are tender. Chopping the cooked greens and serving them on a bed of brown rice makes a very fulfilling meal. Select greens according to your own personal taste. Mustard greens are spicy and strong-tasting. Collards and chard are milder. Drizzle with a little olive oil and garlic or a sprinkling of Annie's Naturals Goddess Dressing or Whole Foods' Sesame Garlic Dressing to give them an out-of-this-world flavor.

Legumes, Tofu, and Grains

Lentils with Spinach

1 $1/3$ cups lentils

3 cups filtered water

3 medium cloves garlic, minced

1 small onion, chopped

1 bay leaf

Sea salt and freshly ground pepper to taste

1 pound fresh organic spinach

$1/2$ teaspoon ground coriander

1 teaspoon ground cumin

Wash and pick over lentils, removing stones and odd-shaped lentils. Combine the lentils, water, two of the minced garlic cloves, onion, and bay leaf in a large saucepan. Bring to a boil. Reduce heat and cover. Add sea salt and freshly ground pepper to taste. Simmer for about 30 minutes or until the lentils are tender. As the lentils cook, stem and wash the spinach. In a large frying pan, wilt the spinach in the water clinging to its leaves. Drain and squeeze out the liquid. Chop the spinach and return to the frying pan. Drain the lentils, retaining about 1 cup of the liquid. Remove the bay leaf. Mix the lentils with the chopped spinach. Add some of the reserved cooking liquid, coriander, cumin, and the remaining minced garlic. Add additional salt and pepper if desired. Mix together over medium heat for 5 minutes and serve immediately. This dish makes an excellent vegetarian protein meal.

Serves 1 to 2.

Refried Beans

2 small onions, chopped

2 cloves garlic, minced

2 tablespoons extra virgin olive oil

2 cups cooked black, pinto, or kidney beans

Sea salt to taste

Cayenne to taste (optional)

Sauté onions and garlic in the olive oil; add the beans, mashing them well. Stir occasionally. Add salt and cayenne as desired. Sauté until crispy. Serve with your favorite vegetables.

Serves 4.

Mung or Adzuki Bean Stew

1 tablespoon organic extra virgin olive oil

$^1/_2$ teaspoon black mustard seeds (optional)

1 large onion, chopped

$^1/_2$ teaspoon turmeric

1 teaspoon ground cumin

1 $^1/_2$ teaspoons ground coriander

1 medium turnip, quartered

1 cup Portobello mushrooms (about 2 large mushrooms), sliced

1 cup cooked mung or adzuki beans

$^1/_4$ cup filtered water or any broth

Sea salt to taste

In a large frying pan, heat the oil, adding the mustard seeds, if desired. Once they start popping, add the chopped onion and lightly brown. Then add the turmeric, cumin, coriander, turnip, and mushrooms and sauté until tender. Pour half of the cooked beans into the pan and stir. Finally, add the water and the remaining beans and mix. Add salt to taste and simmer on low heat for 5 to 10 minutes. Serve over rice or other grains and cooked greens.

Serves 2 to 3.

Pinto or Cannellini Minestrone

1 tablespoon extra virgin olive oil or grapeseed oil

1 pound leeks (white part only), diced

1 cup carrots, diced

1 tablespoon filtered water

6 cups organic vegetable broth

$^1/_2$ cup spelt or rice pasta, shells or elbows

1 tablespoon fresh parsley, chopped

1 tablespoon fresh basil, chopped

2 green onions, coarsely chopped

4 cloves garlic, minced

1 19-ounce can pinto or cannellini beans

1 cup fresh string beans, sliced

1 cup zucchini, diced

1 cup organic frozen green peas

2 cups asparagus, sliced diagonally

Sea salt and freshly ground pepper to taste

In a large soup pot, heat oil over medium heat. Add leeks, carrots, and water. Cover and cook until the leeks are tender. Check frequently for doneness and do not brown. Add the broth and bring to a boil. Add pasta and cook, stirring occasionally, until almost tender. In a small bowl, mix the parsley, basil, green onions, and garlic. Stir into simmering soup. Finally add beans, string beans, zucchini, frozen peas, and asparagus. Cook for 5 more minutes. Season with salt and pepper and serve immediately.

Serves 6.

Bean Dip and Crudités

1 small clove garlic, peeled

1 19-ounce can cannellini beans, rinsed and drained, plus $^1/_2$ cup reserved liquid

$^1/_4$ cup fresh basil

1 tablespoon organic extra virgin olive oil

$^1/_4$ teaspoon dried rosemary

$^1/_4$ teaspoon sea salt

$^1/_4$ teaspoon freshly ground pepper

Fresh vegetables of your choice, for dipping

In a blender, purée the garlic, beans, basil, oil, rosemary, salt, and pepper until well blended. Cover and chill for at least 1 hour. Serve with crudités.

Makes 1 $^1/_4$ cups dip.

Cannellini Beans with Wilted Chard

1 cup dried cannellini beans, rinsed

4 cups cold filtered water

1 bay leaf

2 fresh sage leaves

3 tablespoons organic extra virgin olive oil

Sea salt and freshly ground pepper to taste

4 large cloves garlic, finely chopped

6 cups green chard, coarsely chopped

1 tablespoon organic raw apple cider vinegar

Place beans in a large pot and cover with cold water. Soak overnight. Drain beans and place in a large saucepan. Add 4 cups filtered cold water, the bay leaf, and sage. Bring to a boil over high heat, reduce heat to low, and simmer until beans are very soft, 45 to 60 minutes. Remove the bay and sage leaves, and drain beans if necessary. Using a fork, mash beans.

Stir in 2 tablespoons oil, $^{1}/_{2}$ teaspoon salt, a sprinkling of pepper, and half the garlic. Cover to keep the beans warm. In a large skillet, heat remaining tablespoon of oil over medium heat. Add chard, sprinkle with salt and pepper, and stir to prevent sticking. Sprinkle the vinegar over the chard. When the greens are wilted, remove from heat. Serve the beans on a bed of chard.

Serves 4.

Bean Toasts with Rosemary

$2^{1}/_{2}$ teaspoons organic extra virgin olive oil

2 small cloves garlic, minced

Sea salt and freshly ground pepper to taste

3 slices Ezekiel bread, cut into triangles

$^{2}/_{3}$ cup organic beans of your choice, from a 14-ounce can, rinsed and drained

$^{1}/_{4}$ teaspoon fresh rosemary, finely chopped

Small pinch of crushed red pepper (optional)

Preheat oven to 375°F. In a small bowl, combine 2 teaspoons of the oil with half the garlic. Season with a pinch of salt and pepper. Brush the Ezekiel bread triangles with the seasoned garlic oil and arrange them oiled-side down on a baking sheet. Toast until lightly browned and crisp.

Meanwhile, in a blender, combine the beans, rosemary, and crushed red pepper. Add the remaining garlic and $^{1}/_{2}$ teaspoon oil. Season with salt and blend until smooth. Spoon the bean purée onto the toasts (oiled-side up) and serve immediately.

Serves 2.

Cooked Oriental Tofu

1 pound firm organic tofu
$^1/_2$ cup filtered water
1 tablespoon tamari wheat-free soy sauce
1 teaspoon fresh ginger, grated
6 scallions, with green tops, thinly sliced
2 teaspoons garlic, minced
1 pound fresh organic spinach
Sea salt and freshly ground pepper to taste

Drain tofu and pat dry. Cut tofu into $^1/_2$-inch cubes. Combine tofu, water, tamari, ginger, scallions, and garlic in a large saucepan. Bring to a boil. Simmer for 15 minutes. While the tofu cooks, wash and remove stems from spinach. In a large frying pan, wilt the spinach in the water clinging to its leaves. Remove from heat and drain. Season with sea salt and pepper to taste. Place the spinach on a dish and place tofu on top of it. Serve over brown rice, wheat-free pasta, or other grain. This dish is an excellent vegetarian protein meal.

Serves 3 to 4.

Cold Tofu Salad

1 pound firm organic tofu
4 cups fresh bean sprouts or 1 3.5-ounce package of snow pea shoots
3 to 4 tablespoons Annie's Naturals Shiitake and Sesame Vinaigrette
$^1/_4$ cup scallions, green tops thinly sliced (for garnish)

Drain tofu and pat dry. Cut tofu into 1-inch cubes. Place bean sprouts in a container with the tofu. Slowly drizzle vinaigrette over the mixture. Cover and shake gently to evenly coat the ingredients. Chill until ready to serve. The tofu will absorb the flavor of the dressing and provide a richer taste. When serving, garnish with the sliced scallion tops. If you are lucky enough to find snow pea shoots, prepare the tofu as suggested but combine with the shoots and dressing when you are ready to serve the salad. Then garnish with the scallions. A great choice for a light and refreshing protein meal.

Serves 3 to 4.

Stir-Fried Toasted Rice

3 $^1/_2$ cups filtered water

2 cups uncooked jasmine rice

1 tablespoon expeller-pressed grapeseed oil

1 cup vegetable broth

2 tablespoons tamari wheat-free soy sauce

$^1/_4$ teaspoon crumbled saffron threads

1 tablespoon dried lemon grass

2 tablespoons garlic, finely minced

1 cup fresh mint leaves

1 pound fresh bean sprouts

1 cup scallions, cut in $^1/_4$-inch slices

Boil water and add rice. Cover and simmer until water is absorbed and rice is tender, about 20 minutes. Remove from heat and allow rice to cool for 5 minutes. Fluff rice. Preheat oven to 350°F. Lightly oil a baking sheet. Spread the rice evenly across the sheet, pressing down slightly. Bake for 45 minutes or until the rice forms a slight crust and becomes crispy. In a large pot, heat the broth, tamari, saffron, lemon grass, and garlic until simmering. Remove from heat and add rice, mint, sprouts, and scallions. Stir thoroughly and serve immediately. This dish makes an excellent starch meal.

Serves 4.

Brown Rice Salad

3 cups brown rice, cooked and cooled
1 tablespoon extra virgin olive oil
1 cup fennel bulb, finely diced
$^1/_4$ cup pine nuts
$^1/_4$ cup fresh dill, chopped
$^1/_2$ cup scallions, green tops cut in $^1/_4$-inch slices
$^1/_4$ cup fresh lime juice
Juice of 1 lemon
$^1/_2$ tablespoon raw honey
Sea salt and freshly ground pepper to taste

In a large bowl, toss the rice, olive oil, fennel, pine nuts, dill, and scallions. Shake the lime juice, lemon juice, honey, sea salt, and pepper in a small closed jar until thoroughly blended. Pour over rice mixture, mixing well. This salad can be refrigerated for up to 24 hours.

Serves 4.

Buckwheat (Kasha) Pilaf

1 cup buckwheat groats (kasha)
$1^1/_2$ cups filtered water or vegetable or chicken broth
1 small onion, chopped
1 teaspoon tamari wheat-free soy sauce or Bragg's Liquid Aminos
1 tablespoon olive oil
$^1/_2$ cup frozen peas, steamed (optional)

Place the buckwheat in a pot and cover with water or broth. Stir in the onion and tamari and bring to a boil. Reduce to simmer, cover, and cook until tender, approximately 25 minutes or until all of the water is evaporated and the grains are separate but not soggy. Stir in the olive oil and steamed peas right before serving.

Serves 1 to 2.

Saffron Millet

2 cups millet

4 cups water or vegetable broth

2 tablespoons extra virgin olive oil or grapeseed oil

1 medium onion, chopped

$^1/_2$ teaspoon saffron threads

$^1/_2$ teaspoon ground coriander

$^1/_2$ teaspoon cumin seeds

$^1/_2$ teaspoon ground nutmeg

2 cardamom pods

2 tablespoons slivered almonds

1 tablespoon pine nuts

Cook the millet in 3 $^1/_2$ cups of water for 15 to 20 minutes, or until done. Set aside. Remove the seeds from the cardamom and discard the outer pods. In a separate saucepan, heat the oil and sauté the onion with all the spices for 10 minutes over low heat. Add almonds and pine nuts to spiced onion mixture and sauté gently for 10 minutes or so. Add remaining $^1/_2$ cup water to prevent sticking. Add the spice mixture to the cooked millet and serve immediately.

Serves 4.

Fish

Adele's Asian Adventure with Fish and Veggies

$^1/_2$ pound per person: cod steaks, or scrod or red snapper fillets

2 tablespoons organic extra virgin olive oil

1 large onion, thinly sliced

3 cloves garlic, minced

2 large Portobello mushrooms, sliced

1 cup broccoli florets

1 cup snow peas

1 cup bean sprouts

$^1/_2$ teaspoon curry

$^1/_2$ teaspoon ground cumin

1 tablespoon fresh ginger, grated

Juice of $^1/_2$ lemon

2 teaspoons tamari wheat-free soy sauce

$^1/_2$ cup filtered water

Rinse the fish under cool water and pat dry. Heat the olive oil in a large nonstick sauté pan over medium-high heat. Add the onions, garlic, and mushrooms. Sauté until slightly browned and then add the broccoli, snow peas, and bean sprouts. Cook, continuously tossing for about 1 minute. Add the curry, cumin, and ginger to the mixture and blend thoroughly. Lower heat to simmer and blend in the lemon juice, tamari, and water. Place the raw fish over the mixture and cover pan tightly. Steam fillets for approximately 5 to 8 minutes. If cooking a steak, turn over after 4 minutes and cover with the vegetables. Cook for an additional 4 minutes. Serve immediately.

Serves 2.

Basic Broiled Fish

Broiled fish is an excellent option as a quick, satisfying protein meal. It cooks within minutes and is easy to prepare, but it should be carefully watched for doneness. When fish is overcooked, it can be dry and tasteless.

$^1/_2$ pound per person: cod, grouper, red snapper, or salmon fillets; salmon, swordfish, or tuna steaks

Flavored olive oil spray

Sea salt and freshly ground pepper to taste

$^1/_2$ teaspoon garlic powder or 3 cloves, minced

$^1/_2$ teaspoon sweet paprika or 1 teaspoon dried oregano

$^1/_2$ tablespoon extra virgin olive oil or butter

Lemon wedges (garnish, optional)

Preheat broiler. Rinse fish thoroughly under cool running water. Gently pat dry with a paper towel. Lightly spray pan or dish that you will be using to broil your fish with a flavored olive oil spray of your choice. This will prevent the fish or skin from sticking. Place the fish in the pan. Sprinkle seasonings evenly over entire piece of fish. Dot with olive oil or cut slivers of butter and place about four or five on each piece of fish so it will melt and spread evenly on the surface. Broil for about 4 minutes. Brush the melted butter or oil across the surface of the filet. Continue broiling for approximately 4 minutes. If you are broiling a steak, turn the fish over and brush with the pan juices. Broil for another 4 minutes, checking for doneness. You will know that the fish is cooked properly if it is slightly pink and flakes easily. Salmon and tuna taste best when eaten on the rare side. Remove the fish from the broiler and garnish with a lemon wedge if desired. Fresh lemon juice enhances the flavor of the fish. Serve immediately with a vegetable and salad of your choice.

Broiled Fish with a Zip

1 medium yellow onion, coarsely chopped

2 cloves garlic, minced

1 tablespoon ground coriander

1 tablespoon sweet paprika

$1/4$ cup fresh lemon juice

$1/2$ cup extra virgin olive oil

4 $1/3$ pounds cod, salmon, or swordfish steaks

2 teaspoons fresh oregano, chopped

Sea salt and freshly ground pepper to taste

Place the chopped onion, garlic, coriander, paprika, lemon juice, and olive oil in a blender and purée until smooth. Wash the fish steaks under cool water and pat dry with a paper towel. Place the steaks in a glass or ceramic dish. Pour the puréed mixture over the fish and sprinkle evenly with the oregano. Cover and chill in the refrigerator for at least 2 hours. Preheat broiler. Remove the fish steaks from the dish. Season with salt and pepper. Place the steaks on a broiler pan and broil for about 4 minutes on each side.

Serves 4.

Broiled Fish Kabobs

3 cloves garlic, minced

1 tablespoon ground cumin

3 tablespoons fresh lemon juice

$^3/_4$ teaspoon freshly ground pepper or more if desired

Sea salt to taste

$^1/_3$ cup organic extra virgin olive oil

4 tablespoons fresh mint, chopped

2 tablespoons fresh marjoram, chopped

$1^1/_2$ pounds red snapper, swordfish, or tuna

In a shallow glass or ceramic dish, blend together all of the ingredients, except the fish. Rinse the fish under cool running water and pat dry with a paper towel. Cut into 1-inch cubes. Add the fish cubes to the dish, making sure to thoroughly coat with the mixture. Cover and refrigerate for at least 2 hours. When ready to cook, preheat broiler. Place the cubes onto metal or presoaked wooden skewers. Sprinkle with salt and pepper. Place on a broiling pan and broil for about 2 minutes on each side. Tuna tastes better if cooked medium rare.

Serves 3.

Basic Poached Fish

Fish Stock

1 cup dry white wine

2 cups yellow onions, coarsely chopped

2 celery stalks, chopped

2 strips lemon zest

3 parsley sprigs

1 fresh thyme sprig

5 peppercorns

2 coriander seeds

1 small bay leaf

6 cups filtered water

$^1/_2$ pound per person: cod, red snapper, salmon, or sea bass fillets or steaks

Bring all of the stock ingredients to a boil. Simmer uncovered for about 30 minutes. Strain the stock, let it cool, and then refrigerate. Makes about 2 quarts.

Line a large sauté pan with a piece of cheesecloth. Rinse the fish under cool water and pat dry with a paper towel. When you are ready to poach the fillet, place the fish on top of the piece of cheesecloth, skin-side down. Add enough stock to cover the fish. Bring to a boil. Lower heat, cover, and simmer for about 8 to 10 minutes for a 1-inch-thick fillet. When fish is opaque throughout, gently lift the fillet out of the stock and let cool. Flip the fillet over, slipping it onto a large platter so that the skin side is up. Remove the skin. Serve at room temperature or chill. The following recipe for aioli sauce goes especially well with poached fish. Serve with lightly steamed vegetables, and you will have a delectable meal.

Aioli Sauce

2 organic egg yolks, at room temperature

2 tablespoons garlic, finely minced

1 teaspoon Dijon or stone-ground mustard

1 cup organic extra virgin olive oil

$1^1/_2$ teaspoons fresh lemon juice

Sea salt and freshly ground pepper to taste

In a mixing bowl, beat the egg yolks until pale in color. Whisk in the garlic and mustard. Slowly drizzle in the olive oil, beating constantly. When the sauce begins to thicken, stir in the lemon juice. Continue to slowly drizzle the olive oil into the sauce. When the sauce becomes thick, stop adding the oil. Season the sauce with sea salt and pepper to taste. When preparing ahead of time, cover and refrigerate.

Makes about 1 $^1/_3$ cups.

Baked Tandoori Fish

1 small onion, coarsely chopped

1 clove garlic, chopped, per fish fillet

2 tablespoons fresh ginger, thinly sliced

2 tablespoons fresh lime juice

2 teaspoons ground coriander

1 teaspoon ground cumin

$^1/_4$ teaspoon ground cardamom

1 tablespoon sweet paprika

$^1/_2$ teaspoon sea salt

1 cup organic plain low-fat yogurt

$^1/_2$ pound per person: cod, red snapper, or sea bass fillets

2 tablespoons fresh cilantro, chopped (for garnish)

In a blender, combine the onion, garlic, ginger, and lime juice. Purée. Add the spices and yogurt and continue to purée until smooth. Wash the fish fillets under cool water and pat dry with a paper towel. Place them in a glass or ceramic dish and pour the puréed mixture to cover the fillets. Cover and refrigerate for about 4 hours. Allow the fish to return to room temperature. Preheat oven to 450°F. Remove the fillets from the marinade mixture and place in a baking dish. Make sure that the fillets are lying flat in a single layer. Bake for about 8 minutes or until fish is opaque. Garnish with the cilantro and serve immediately.

Giovanna's Sautéed Tuna

4 large yellow onions, thinly sliced

4 to 6 tablespoons organic extra virgin olive oil

1 tablespoon balsamic vinegar (optional)

$1^1/_2$ cups rice or spelt flour

Sea salt and freshly ground pepper to taste

4 tuna steaks, $^1/_2$ pound each, about 1-inch thick

In a large nonstick frying pan, sauté the onions in 2 tablespoons of the olive oil, over medium to low heat, until they are golden brown. Add balsamic vinegar if desired. Remove the onions from the pan and reserve. In a flat container, blend together the flour, salt, and pepper. Rinse the tuna steaks and dredge in the flour. In the same pan that you sautéed the onions in, add 2 more tablespoons of olive oil and sauté the tuna steaks over medium-high heat, browning on both sides. Add additional olive oil if necessary to prevent sticking. Check for doneness. Tuna should be slightly rare or pink in the middle when served.

Serves 4.

Seared Tuna with Sautéed Fennel

2 tablespoons organic extra virgin olive oil

2 cloves garlic, pressed

4 small fennel bulbs, thinly sliced

Sea salt and freshly ground pepper to taste

4 tuna steaks, $1/2$ pound each, about 1-inch thick

1 tablespoon fresh parsley, finely chopped

4 lemon wedges (for garnish)

Heat the olive oil over low heat in a large nonstick pan. Add the garlic and cook until transparent. Add the fennel, salt, and pepper. Cover and simmer over low heat for 10 minutes or until the fennel is tender. Stir occasionally to avoid sticking. Remove pan from heat and set aside. Rinse the tuna steaks under cool water and pat dry with a paper towel. Lightly salt and pepper the steaks and cook in another nonstick pan over medium-high heat. Sear for about 45 seconds on each side. Place the tuna steaks on top of the fennel in the other pan. Cover the pan and place over medium heat for about 1 minute. Turn steaks and cook for an additional minute. Check for doneness. The steaks should be pink in the middle. Be careful not to overcook, or the tuna will be dry. Sprinkle with parsley, garnish with lemon wedges, and serve immediately.

Serves 4.

Poultry and Meat

Turkey or Chicken Cutlets with Lemon

1 $1/2$ pounds organic turkey or chicken cutlets

2 cups spelt flour

Sea salt and white pepper to taste

2 tablespoons organic extra virgin olive oil

$3/4$ cup chicken broth

$1/4$ cup dry white wine

1 tablespoon fresh lemon juice

1 fresh lemon, sliced thin

2 tablespoons fresh parsley, finely minced

Rinse the turkey (or chicken) cutlets in cool water. In a flat-sided container or dish, blend together the flour with the salt and pepper. Dredge the cutlets in the seasoned flour, making sure to coat them thoroughly. Heat the olive oil in a large nonstick frying pan, brown the cutlets on both sides over medium-high heat, and remove to a serving platter. Add the broth, wine, and lemon juice to the frying pan. Return the cutlets to the pan and place one slice of lemon in the center of each cutlet. Lower heat and continuously baste with the sauce. When the sauce reduces and thickens, the cutlets are ready to serve. Drizzle the remaining sauce over each serving and sprinkle with the fresh parsley.

Serves 4.

Garlic- and Basil-Infused Turkey Breast

2 tablespoons organic extra virgin olive oil

1 large clove garlic, pressed

$1/4$ teaspoon sea salt

$1/8$ teaspoon freshly ground pepper

1 whole organic turkey breast, any size

1 bunch fresh basil

$^{1}/_{2}$ cup filtered water

1 cup dry white wine

5 unpeeled cloves garlic

Preheat oven to 325°F. In a bowl, thoroughly blend the olive oil, pressed garlic clove, salt, and pepper. Rinse the turkey breast under cool running water and pat dry with a paper towel. Gently lift the skin and pull it back to expose the breast meat. Brush the breast meat with the oil mixture. Cover the surface with fresh basil leaves. Carefully replace the skin on the breast. Be careful not to tear the skin during this process. Brush the skin with the remaining oil mixture. Add the water, wine, and unpeeled garlic cloves to a baking pan. Place the breast in the pan and roast for approximately 18 minutes per pound. Remove the turkey from the oven and let it stand for at least 10 minutes before carving. The number of servings depends on the size of the turkey breast.

Grilled Turkey Tenderloins

1 medium onion, grated

Juice of 1 large lemon

1 tablespoon organic extra virgin olive oil

3 cloves garlic, pressed

1 tablespoon ground coriander

$^{1}/_{8}$ teaspoon sea salt

4 grinds of fresh pepper

6 organic turkey tenderloins, about $^{1}/_{2}$ pound each

Grate the onion and discard its juice. In a glass or ceramic dish, blend together the drained onion, lemon juice, olive oil, garlic, coriander, salt, and pepper. Rinse the turkey tenderloins under cool water and pat them dry with a paper towel. Place the tenderloins into the dish with the marinade and thoroughly coat each one. Cover the dish and refrigerate for at least 3 hours. Grill or broil the tenderloins for about 5 minutes on each side. Check for doneness by making sure that the meat is no longer pink in the center. Serve with Curry Mayonnaise (recipe on page 74) and Cucumber and Yogurt Raita (recipe on page 86).

Serves 6.

Turkey Moussaka

3 3/4 pounds zucchini

Sea salt to taste

3 tablespoons organic butter or organic extra virgin olive oil

1 1/2 pounds organic ground turkey

3/4 cup yellow onion, chopped

1 tablespoon tomato paste

2 tablespoons fresh parsley, chopped

1/4 cup white wine

Sea salt and freshly ground pepper to taste

1/4 cup filtered water

1/8 teaspoon cinnamon

1/4 cup Romano or soy Parmesan cheese, grated

1/4 cup spelt or Ezekiel bread crumbs

3 tablespoons spelt or rice flour

1 1/2 cups hot soy milk

1/4 teaspoon sea salt

1/8 teaspoon pepper, or to taste

1/8 teaspoon ground nutmeg

1 extra large organic egg, lightly beaten

Extra virgin olive oil, for brushing on zucchini

Cut the zucchini lengthwise into 1/2-inch slices. Place the pieces on a large tray that is lined with absorbent paper towels and sprinkle the zucchini lightly with sea salt. Place another layer of paper towels over the zucchini and then weighted plates on top of the towels. Let the zucchini stand for about 30 minutes, and then rinse and dry the zucchini.

Melt 1 tablespoon of the butter or oil in a nonstick saucepan and sauté the turkey and the onions until the turkey is thoroughly cooked through. Add the tomato paste, parsley, wine, sea salt, pepper, and water.

Simmer the mixture until the liquid has been absorbed. Remove from the heat and cool. Stir in the cinnamon, half of the cheese, and half of the bread crumbs.

To prepare the sauce:

Melt the remaining 2 tablespoons of the butter or oil in a saucepan over low heat. Add the flour and whisk until blended. Remove the mixture from the heat and gradually whisk in the soy milk. Return the sauce to the heat and cook, whisking until the sauce is thick and smooth. Add sea salt, pepper, and nutmeg. Combine the egg with a little of the warm sauce and then stir the egg mixture into the sauce and cook it over very low heat for 2 minutes. Stir the sauce constantly.

Preheat the broiler. Lightly brush the zucchini slices with the olive oil on both sides. Place the slices on an ungreased cookie sheet and broil them until they are lightly browned. Set the zucchini aside to cool.

Preheat the oven to 350°F. Sprinkle the bottom of an 8 x 8-inch baking dish or pan with the remaining bread crumbs. Place a layer of zucchini slices on the bread crumbs, then spread the turkey mixture over the zucchini. Cover the meat with the remaining zucchini slices, and spoon the sauce over all. Sprinkle with the remaining cheese.

Bake for 40 minutes, or until it is golden brown. Cool for at least 10 minutes before cutting it to serve. Moussaka can be frozen and reheated.

Serves 6.

Basic Broiled Chicken

2$^1/_2$ to 3 pounds organic broiler chicken

Sea salt and freshly ground pepper to taste

$^1/_2$ teaspoon garlic powder or more if desired

$^1/_2$ teaspoon sweet paprika or more if desired

Place oven rack approximately 10 inches from the source of heat. Preheat broiler. Split chicken in half and wash thoroughly under cold water. Line the bottom part of a broiler pan with aluminum foil to catch the grease from the chicken. Place the chicken skin-side up on the top portion of the broiler pan. Season with spices, making sure to evenly coat the surface. Broil for approximately 10 minutes, watching closely to make sure the chicken doesn't char or burn. Turn chicken halves over, season, and broil for 10 minutes more. Bake chicken at 375°F for an additional 10 minutes. A Caesar Salad (recipe on page 69) complements this dish.

Serves 4.

Marinated Broiled Chicken

1 tablespoon fresh ginger, chopped

1 teaspoon fresh garlic, finely minced

$^1/_4$ cup fresh lemon juice

1$^1/_2$ tablespoons organic extra virgin olive oil

1 bay leaf, broken into small pieces

$^1/_2$ teaspoon dried thyme

Sea salt and freshly ground pepper to taste

2$^1/_2$- to 3-pound organic broiler chicken

In a large lidded container, combine the ginger, garlic, lemon juice, olive oil, bay leaf, thyme, sea salt, and pepper. Place the chicken in the container, cover, and shake to evenly coat the pieces. Refrigerate for at least 2 hours before broiling. Follow directions for Basic Broiled Chicken (recipe on page 110). Broil skin-side up until nicely browned, or about 10 minutes. Baste both sides with the marinade, turn, and broil for an additional 10 minutes. Set oven temperature to 350°F and bake for 10 minutes more.

Serves 4.

Broiled Chicken with Mustard

2$^1/_2$- to 3-pound organic broiler chicken, split in half

1$^1/_2$ tablespoons organic extra virgin olive oil

2 tablespoons Dijon or stone-ground mustard

Sea salt and freshly ground pepper to taste

Follow directions for Basic Broiled Chicken (recipe on page 110). Brush chicken thoroughly to coat with the olive oil and then the mustard. Sprinkle each half with salt and pepper. Broil for approximately 10 minutes or until chicken browns; turn the pieces over and baste with the remaining oil and mustard. Broil for another 10 minutes. Bake the chicken for an additional 10 minutes in a 350°F oven.

Serves 4.

Roasted Chicken with Herbs

2 1/2- to 3-pound organic broiler chicken

2 tablespoons organic butter, melted

Sea salt to taste

Lemon pepper to taste

1/2 teaspoon ground sage

4 cloves garlic, minced

2 teaspoons dried basil

2 teaspoons dried thyme

Preheat oven to 350°F. Wash the chicken under cool running water and make sure to thoroughly clean the cavity. Pat the surface and cavity dry with a paper towel. Brush the entire surface of the chicken with the butter. Sprinkle the salt, lemon pepper, sage, garlic, basil, and thyme over the chicken. Secure the wings and legs of the chicken to the body with cooking string. Place the chicken in a roasting pan and roast, uncovered, for 1 1/4 hours. The chicken is done when its juices run clear after piercing with a fork. Cover the chicken and allow to stand for at least 10 minutes before carving.

Serves 4.

Sautéed Chicken with Fresh Rosemary

2 split organic chicken breasts

1 tablespoon organic butter

Sea salt and freshly ground pepper to taste

1 teaspoon fresh rosemary, finely chopped

1 tablespoon shallots, finely chopped

2 tablespoons dry white wine

$^1/_2$ cup organic chicken broth

Wash the chicken pieces under cool running water and pat dry with a paper towel. Melt the butter over medium-high heat in a large sauté pan that can hold all of the pieces of chicken. Sprinkle the salt and pepper over the chicken. Place the chicken in the pan skin-side down and brown for 15 minutes. Turn the pieces, sprinkle with the rosemary, and sauté for an additional 10 minutes over medium heat. Remove the chicken to a serving platter. Pour off the butter and fat from the pan and add the shallots. Cook for 30 seconds, add the wine, and then add the broth. Return the chicken to the pan. Baste it with the sauce. Lower the heat, cover pan, and simmer for 10 minutes. Pour the sauce over each piece of chicken.

Serves 4.

Teriyaki Chicken

$^1/_2$ cup tamari wheat-free soy sauce

2 teaspoons grapeseed oil

$^1/_4$ cup dry sherry

1 tablespoon Sucanat sugar

2 tablespoons grated onion

2 large cloves garlic, pressed

2 split organic chicken breasts

Place the first four marinade ingredients in a pan and heat until the Sucanat is dissolved. Do not let boil. Pour the marinade into a glass or ceramic dish over the grated onion and pressed garlic cloves and let cool. Rinse the chicken pieces under cold water and pat them dry with a paper towel. Place the chicken into the dish with the marinade and thoroughly coat each piece. Cover the dish and refrigerate for at least 3 hours. Grill or broil the split breasts for 8 minutes on each side. Then bake the chicken for an additional 15 minutes at 350°F. Check for doneness by making sure that the meat is no longer pink in the center.

Serves 4.

> When selecting red meat for a meal, lamb is a better option than beef, as it is digested more easily.

Herb-Crusted Roast Leg of Lamb

One organic leg of lamb, shank portion or a boneless roast

1 tablespoon organic extra virgin olive oil or grapeseed oil

Sea salt to taste

$^1/_2$ teaspoon garlic powder

Freshly ground pepper to taste

$^1/_2$ teaspoon each dried sage, thyme, and rosemary

Preheat oven to 350°F. Gently rinse the leg of lamb under cool water and pat dry with a paper towel. Brush the entire surface of the roast with the oil. Coat all sides of the lamb with each of the spices, in the order that they are indicated. Roast lamb for 30 minutes per pound, but check for doneness about a half hour before anticipated finish time. If you prefer the meat on the rare side, you can slice the meat around the outside portion of the leg, then return it to the oven to complete the roasting of the rarer meat that surrounds the bone. Slice the remaining meat and serve immediately. Figure approximately $^1/_2$ pound per person, if there is a bone; $^1/_4$ pound if not.

Broiled Boneless Butterflied Leg of Lamb

1 organic boneless butterflied leg of lamb

1 tablespoon grapeseed oil

Sea salt to taste

1 teaspoon garlic powder or more to taste

Freshly ground pepper to taste

2 tablespoons Dijon or stone-ground mustard

2 teaspoons each dried sage, thyme, and rosemary

Preheat broiler. Gently rinse the lamb under cool water and pat dry with a paper towel. Line the bottom portion of a broiler pan with aluminum foil to catch the fatty drippings. Place the meat on the upper portion of the broiler pan. Brush with the oil, and coat evenly with the salt, garlic powder, and freshly ground pepper. Broil for about 7 minutes. Turn the meat and brush with the oil and then the mustard to coat the surface. Evenly sprinkle the lamb with the sage, thyme, and rosemary. Broil for about 7 minutes and check for doneness. Lamb is done based upon personal preference. Some like it rarer than others. Remove the lamb from the broiler and let it stand for about 10 minutes before slicing. Slice and serve immediately. Serving size is 4 to 6 ounces per person.

Broiled Mustard London Broil or Steak

1 lean organic London broil or steak

Sea salt to taste

$1/2$ teaspoon garlic powder

Freshly ground pepper to taste

1 tablespoon Dijon or stone ground mustard

Preheat the broiler. Rinse the meat under cool water and pat dry with a paper towel. Line a broiler pan with aluminum foil to catch the fatty drippings. Place the meat on the upper portion of the broiler pan. Sprinkle evenly with the salt, garlic powder, and freshly ground pepper. Broil for 5 minutes on one side. Turn the meat over and brush to coat the surface with the mustard. Broil for another 5 minutes and check whether it is as rare or as well done as you like it. Serving size is 4 to 6 ounces per person.

Pasta and Pizza

Spelt Pasta with Pesto Sauce

1 cup fresh basil leaves, tightly packed

1 large clove garlic

1 tablespoon pine nuts

$1/4$ cup organic extra virgin olive oil

2 tablespoons freshly grated Romano or soy Parmesan cheese

Sea salt to taste

1 pound Vita spelt or rice pasta

Place the basil, garlic, and pine nuts in a blender. Whirl until finely chopped. While the blender is running, slowly add the oil in a thin stream. Scrape down the sides and make sure that the sauce is smooth. Add the cheese and sea salt and blend well. Serve over freshly cooked spelt or rice pasta. This sauce can be made and stored for up to one month in a sealed container in the refrigerator. Do not heat this sauce in the microwave. The recipe yields approximately $1/2$ cup of sauce.

Boil 2 quarts of water in a large pot and add the pasta. Cook 5 to 7 minutes, stirring occasionally. Taste for preferred doneness. Drain and rinse, if desired. Blend in the pesto sauce and serve immediately.

Serves 4 to 6.

Oriental Rice or Spelt Noodles

$1/4$ teaspoon sea salt

8 ounces spelt or rice angel hair pasta

1 tablespoon organic extra virgin olive oil

$1/2$ cup bean sprouts

1 tablespoon tamari wheat-free soy sauce

1 teaspoon organic rice vinegar

$1/4$ teaspoon red pepper flakes

8 cups filtered water

$^1/_2$ teaspoon Sucanat sugar

2 cloves garlic, minced

2 scallions, sliced diagonally

$^1/_2$ teaspoon raw sesame seeds

In a pasta pot, bring 8 cups of filtered water to a boil. When water boils, add salt and pasta. Stir to prevent sticking. Cook according to package directions until al dente. Drain, rinse under cold running water, and then drain well. Place noodles in a bowl, tossing with the olive oil. Cover and refrigerate until chilled, or keep warm if desired to be served hot.

Meanwhile, blanch bean sprouts in boiling water for 30 seconds. Drain and transfer to a large bowl. Add remaining ingredients and mix well. Add either cold or hot noodles, tossing to coat thoroughly, and serve immediately.

Serves 2 to 3.

Spelt Fusilli with Garlicky Greens

1 pound bunch of greens (dandelion, spinach, or escarole)

1 tablespoon sea salt

12 ounces spelt fusilli pasta

2 tablespoons organic extra virgin olive oil

6 cloves garlic, minced

$^1/_2$ cup feta cheese

Cayenne pepper to taste (optional)

Bring water to a boil in a large pot with a steamer basket insert. Add the greens and steam for 5 minutes. Remove steamer basket with greens. Add additional water to the pot and return to a boil. Add salt and pasta, cooking according to package directions until al dente.

Meanwhile, squeeze excess water from greens and chop. In large nonstick skillet, heat oil over medium heat. Add garlic and cook, stirring often, for 30 seconds. Add chopped greens and cook until heated through.

Drain cooked pasta and return to the pot. Add greens and garlic; toss to mix. Transfer to serving bowl. Crumble feta cheese over pasta and sprinkle with a small amount of cayenne pepper if desired. Serve immediately.

Serves 4.

Cold or Hot Rice Noodles with Peanut Sauce

2 cloves garlic, minced

1 tablespoon fresh ginger, peeled and grated

2 scallions, white and pale green parts, chopped

2 tablespoons organic peanut butter

2 tablespoons tahini

2 teaspoons tamari wheat-free soy sauce

2 tablespoons organic rice vinegar

2 tablespoons sesame seeds, toasted

$1/4$ cup hot water

1 pound rice pasta, spaghetti style

Bring a large pot of water to a boil. Meanwhile, in a blender, combine all of the ingredients except for the rice pasta and process until it has a smooth consistency. Transfer the sauce to a large bowl.

When the water boils, add the rice pasta and stir to prevent sticking. Cook the spaghetti according to the package directions until al dente. Drain, rinse under cold running water, and drain again.

Transfer the noodles to the bowl with the sauce and toss to coat. Either serve immediately or cover and refrigerate until the mixture is thoroughly chilled, at least 3 hours. Toss again just before serving.

Serves 4.

Spelt Pizza Variations

Place a spelt pita on a cookie sheet. Toast one side of the pita under the broiler on the lowest shelf from the broiling element. Watch carefully until it is lightly browned. Remove from the broiler. Turn the pita over and select a topping from the following choices:

- Pesto sauce with fresh mozzarella cheese
- Millina's Finest Organic Sauce with soy cheese
- Garlic Basil Chavrie (goat cheese) on top of steamed spinach

Place the sauce and then the cheese on the pita, leaving about a 3/4-inch rim around the edges of the pita free of the topping. Return the pizza to the lowest shelf of the broiler and heat until the rim of the pita has browned. Remove the pizza from the broiler and let it cool for a few minutes. If using the goat cheese as your topping, allow the cheese to turn golden brown before removing the pizza from the broiler.

Serves 1 to 2.

Desserts and Snacks

The best time to indulge in a dessert or snack is during the late afternoon. If you select a fresh fruit or fruit salad, be sure to eat it 15 minutes prior to a meal or 1 hour after a meal. Juicing fresh organic vegetables or fruits can boost energy levels and reduce a nagging feeling of hunger. There are also a variety of fresh juices available in natural food stores. One fourth cup of a nut compatible with your blood type is also a great energy-promoting snack. Yogurt or a rice cracker spread with almond or peanut butter makes a very satisfying choice, if compatible with your blood type.

Simple No-Cook Choices *(individual choices should be compatible with your blood type)*

- Fresh vegetable or fruit juice
- Nuts ($^1/_4$ cup)
- Fresh fruit or fruit salad

- Plain or fruit juice–sweetened organic yogurt
- Rice crackers spread with almond or peanut butter

Any of the following desserts should be eaten in moderation—once or twice a week. Remember, the less sugar you eat, the faster the pounds will roll off—and stay off.

Desserts

Peaches in White Wine

6 large organic peaches, peeled, stoned, and sliced

Organic white wine, to cover

2 tablespoons Sucanat sugar

Arrange the peaches in a bowl. Pour on enough wine to cover and sprinkle with Sucanat. Let macerate for 1 hour or up to 12 hours.

Serves 6.

Just Custard

2 cups soy milk or 1 $^1/_2$ cups rice milk

$^1/_4$ cup Sucanat sugar

$^1/_8$ teaspoon sea salt

4 organic egg yolks, beaten

1 teaspoon vanilla or 1 tablespoon grated lemon rind

$^1/_8$ teaspoon nutmeg

Preheat oven to 325°F. Blend together the milk, sugar, and salt. Add the egg yolks and beat well. Add the vanilla (or lemon rind) and nutmeg. When this is all well beaten, pour into individual custard cups. Place the cups in a pan of water in the oven for 1 hour. Refrigerate and serve when thoroughly chilled.

Serves 3 to 4.

Raspberry Mousse

$^1/_2$ cup organic berry nectar

1 tablespoon agar-agar flakes

12 3-ounce packages soft silken tofu

3 cups fresh raspberries

1 $^1/_2$ tablespoons raw honey or brown rice syrup

1 teaspoon vanilla extract

In a small saucepan, bring berry nectar to a simmer over low heat. Add agar-agar and stir until dissolved. In a blender, combine nectar mixture, tofu, raspberries, honey (or brown rice syrup), and vanilla. Process until almost smooth. Pour into 4 dessert dishes. Chill at least 1 hour.

Serves 4.

Pineapple Sorbet

1 ripe pineapple (about 4 pounds)

1 tablespoon fructose sweetener or to taste

5 tablespoons fresh organic lemon juice

1 large organic egg white, slightly beaten

Trim off the top and the bottom of the pineapple. Cut the pineapple in half and then into quarters. Slice along the bottom portion of each piece, separating the flesh of the pineapple from the outer skin. Dig out any brown fibrous eyes. Remove any woody flesh along the peak of each quarter.

Purée the pineapple in a food processor. Add the fructose sweetener and the lemon juice and blend. If it is too tart for your taste, adjust by adding more fructose sweetener.

Place the purée in an ice-cream freezer and follow the manufacturer's instructions. When the mixture begins to freeze, add the egg white and continue freezing.

Serves 6.

Poached Pears with Ginger

2 cups filtered water

6 pears, peeled, halved, and cored

1 tablespoon fructose sweetener

$^1/_8$ teaspoon ginger

1 slice organic lemon

In a large saucepan, bring the water to a simmer and poach the pears for 10 minutes. Add the fructose sweetener, ginger, and lemon and continue poaching for 15 minutes or until tender. Discard the lemon slice and chill before serving. For best results, this simple dessert can be prepared 2 days in advance.

Serves 6.

Poached Apples 'n' Spice

4 apples, preferably Rome variety

$^1/_2$ cup dry red wine

1 cup filtered water

$^1/_4$ cup Sucanat sugar

1 bay leaf

$^1/_4$ teaspoon peppercorns

6 whole allspice

6 whole cloves

1 cinnamon stick, 2-inches in length

Peel the apples, but leave the stems on. Use an apple corer to cut out the center of each apple from the bottom, but do not ream the apples all the way to the stem end.

Combine the remaining ingredients in a saucepan and add the apples. Bring everything to a boil and then let it simmer about 10 minutes, turning the apples occasionally in the syrup so that they cook evenly. If desired, remove the apples and cook down the syrup by half. Return the apples to the sauce. Turn off the heat and let everything stand until you are ready to serve. These apples are delicious when eaten warm or cold.

Serves 4.

Carrot Cake

$1/2$ cup raisins

Filtered water, to cover

1 cup walnuts, coarsely chopped

3 cups spelt flour

1 tablespoon baking powder

2 teaspoons baking soda

2 teaspoons ground cinnamon

$1/4$ teaspoon sea salt

1 teaspoon ground allspice

$3/4$ teaspoon ground nutmeg

1 cup brown rice syrup

$1/4$ cup grapeseed oil

$1/4$ cup soy or rice milk

2 teaspoons vanilla extract

1 tablespoon raw apple cider vinegar

3 cups organic carrots, finely grated

Preheat oven to 350°F. Grease a 10-inch tube pan. In a cup, combine raisins and enough filtered warm water to cover and let soak for 20 minutes. Meanwhile, spread walnuts in a baking pan and bake for 5 to 10 minutes until toasted, stirring once. Remove from oven. In a large bowl, sift spelt flour, baking powder, baking soda, cinnamon, salt, allspice, and nutmeg. In another large bowl, stir together rice syrup, oil, soy or rice milk, vanilla extract, and vinegar. Sprinkle grated carrots into flour mixture and mix until well coated. Gradually add liquid mixture, stirring with wooden spoon. Drain raisins and stir into batter along with toasted walnuts (batter will be stiff). Spoon batter into prepared pan, spreading evenly. Bake until cake pulls away from sides of pan and is firm with a little spring to the touch (45 to 60 minutes). Let cool 20 minutes in pan. To remove from pan, run knife around edge of pan and turn cake out onto wire rack. Cool completely before removing from tube.

Serves 12.

Almond Meringues

1 cup organic almonds

3 organic egg whites

$1/4$ teaspoon cream of tartar

$1/8$ teaspoon ground nutmeg

$1/8$ teaspoon ground cinnamon

5 tablespoons fructose sweetener

1 teaspoon vanilla extract

Preheat oven to 350°F. Spread almonds in a shallow pan. Bake 5 to 10 minutes until lightly browned. Let nuts cool and then chop finely. Reduce oven temperature to 300°F. Line baking sheet with wax paper. In a medium bowl, combine egg whites, cream of tartar, nutmeg, and cinnamon. Using electric mixer, beat at high speed until foamy. Gradually add fructose, beating until mixture is stiff and glossy. Using a rubber spatula, gently fold in vanilla extract and almonds. Drop rounded teaspoons onto prepared baking sheets, spacing about 2 inches apart. Bake until cookies feel firm when touched lightly, about 25 minutes. Remove to wire racks and let cool. Store in an airtight container at room temperature for up to 3 days.

Makes 50 cookies.

Recipe Conversions

Green Stevia powder*
1 cup white sugar can be replaced with $1\frac{1}{2}$ to 2 tablespoons stevia

White Stevia powder (much sweeter than green stevia leaf powder)
1 cup of white sugar can be replaced with $1/4$ teaspoon stevia

* *Sweetening effect varies depending on the brand and grade used.*

Yummy Brownies

$^2/_3$ cup spelt flour

4 tablespoons nondairy hot chocolate powder

$1^1/_2$ teaspoons baking powder (aluminum-free)

$1^1/_2$ teaspoons white stevia powder

$^1/_8$ teaspoon salt (optional)

$^1/_3$ cup grapeseed oil or organic unsweetened applesauce

$^1/_3$ cup filtered or bottled water

2 organic eggs, lightly beaten

$^1/_2$ tablespoon vanilla extract

1 cup chopped nuts of your choice

$^1/_2$ cup chocolate or carob chips (optional)

Preheat oven to 350°F. Thoroughly mix together the first five ingredients. Add oil (or applesauce), water, eggs, and vanilla. Mix well. Add remaining ingredients. Stir well until mixed. Pour into greased 8-by-8-inch pan. Bake 20 minutes or until toothpick inserted comes out clean.

Makes 16 brownies.

Muffins

Cooked Oatmeal Muffins

2 organic eggs, separated

1 cup cooked organic oatmeal

$1^1/_4$ cups soy or rice milk

2 tablespoons organic butter or soy margarine, melted

$1^1/_2$ cups spelt flour

1 tablespoon Sucanat sugar

$^1/_2$ teaspoon sea salt

2 teaspoons baking powder

Preheat oven to 400°F. Beat the two egg yolks and add the oatmeal, milk, and butter. Sift the flour and resift with the sugar, salt, and baking powder. Beat the two egg whites until stiff. Combine the liquid and the dry ingredients with a few swift strokes, then fold in the egg whites. Fill muffin tins that have been lined with paper baking cups two-thirds full. Bake for 20 to 25 minutes or until done.

Makes about 15 4-inch muffins.

Blueberry Muffins

$2^{1}/_{3}$ cups spelt flour

1 teaspoon baking powder

$^{1}/_{2}$ teaspoon sea salt

1 teaspoon ground cinnamon

$^{1}/_{2}$ cup Sucanat sugar

$^{1}/_{4}$ cup grapeseed oil

2 organic eggs

1 teaspoon vanilla extract

$^{3}/_{4}$ cup soy or rice milk

1 cup fresh blueberries

Preheat oven to 375°F. Mix together the flour, baking powder, salt, cinnamon, and sugar. In a separate bowl, mix the oil, eggs, vanilla extract, and milk. Combine both mixtures, being careful not to overmix (about 10 strokes will do it). Gently blend in blueberries. Fill muffin tins that have been lined with paper baking cups two-thirds full. Bake for 12 to 15 minutes or until done.

Makes 12 4-inch muffins.

Cranberry Muffins

2 cups spelt flour

$^1/_2$ cup walnuts

$^1/_2$ teaspoon ginger powder

1 cup rice flour

2 organic eggs

$^1/_2$ cup maple syrup

1 cup organic 1% milk or soy milk

1 tablespoon grapeseed oil

$^1/_2$ cup dried cranberries (or currants)

Preheat oven to 400°F. Blend dry ingredients in a bowl. Beat liquids together in a separate bowl. Add dry mixture to liquids and stir well. Fold the cranberries or currants into the batter. Divide into oiled muffin tins or paper baking cups and bake for 20 minutes or until done.

Makes 12 4-inch muffins.

Rice Flour Muffins

1 cup rice flour

$^1/_2$ teaspoon sea salt

2 teaspoons baking powder

1 tablespoon Sucanat sugar

2 tablespoons organic butter or soy margarine

1 organic egg, well beaten

1 cup soy or rice milk or 1% organic milk

2 tablespoons organic raisins

Preheat oven to 450°F. In a medium bowl, mix together the flour, salt, baking powder, and sugar. Melt butter or margarine and remove from heat. When slightly cooled, add to the egg and milk. With a few light strokes, combine the dry ingredients with the liquid mixture. Add raisins and pour into paper-lined muffin tins until two-thirds full. Bake for 12 to 15 minutes or until done.

Makes 12 4-inch muffins.

Blueberry Oatmeal Muffins

1 cup spelt flour

1 cup rolled oats

$^{1}/_{8}$ teaspoon salt (optional)

3 teaspoons baking powder (aluminum-free)

$^{1}/_{8}$ teaspoon ground nutmeg

$1^{1}/_{2}$ teaspoons white stevia powder

1 egg

$^{3}/_{4}$ cup soy milk or 1% organic cow's milk

$^{1}/_{4}$ cup grapeseed oil or organic unsweetened applesauce

$^{3}/_{4}$ cup blueberries, or currants, or raisins

Preheat the oven to 400°F. Mix the flour, oats, salt, baking powder, nutmeg, stevia powder, and egg thoroughly. In a separate bowl, mix milk, oil (or applesauce), and blueberries (or currants or raisins). Gradually mix dry ingredients with moist ingredients. Spoon into greased muffin tins or into paper baking cups two-thirds full. Bake for 15 to 20 minutes or until done.

Makes 12 4-inch muffins.

Appendix:
Preferred Products List

The following is a partial list of recommended products, many of which are available at your local health-food stores.

Products	Manufacturer
Organic, allergy-free, and kosher/parve products; soy products; and salt-free products	Eden Foods Inc. 701 Tecumseh Road Clinton, MI 49236-9599 (517) 456-7424 Fax: (571) 456-6075 E-mail: sales@eden-foods.com
Organic, allergy-free, and kosher/parve products; soy products; and salt-free products; brown rice snaps	Edward & Sons Trading Co. P.O. Box 1326 Carpinteria, CA 93014-1326 (805) 684-8500 Fax: (805) 684-8220 E-mail: edwardsons@aol.com
Ezekiel sprouted grain bread (plain or cinnamon raisin), rice pasta, baked products/breads, sweeteners, kosher/parve products, and rice products	Food For Life Baking Co., Inc. 2991 East Dougherty Street Corona, CA 91719 (909) 279-5090 or 1-800-797-5090 Fax: (909) 279-1784 E-mail: info@food-for-life.com
Full line of organic products including Ezekiel sprouted bagels, baked goods/breads, wheat/yeast-free products, kosher/parve products, and macrobiotic products	French Meadow Bakery, Inc. 2610 Lyndale Avenue South Minneapolis, MN 55408-1321 (612) 870-4740 Fax: (612) 870-0907 E-mail: bread@frenchmeadow.com

Products	Manufacturer
Wheat/yeast-free products, pack-aged baking mixes, specialty/gourmet products, rice products, and packaged convenience foods	Gluten-Free Pantry 77 Kreiger Lane #902 Glastonbury, CT 06033-2371 (860) 633-3826 Fax: (860) 633-6853 E-mail: pantry@glutenfree.com
Organic Japanese green tea, refrigerated/frozen soy products, packaged pasta, condiments, spices, seasonings, macrobiotic products, and kosher/parve products	Great Eastern Sun 92 Mcintosh Road Asheville, NC 28806-1406 1-800-334-5809 Fax: (828) 667-8051 E-mail: salesmgr@great-eastern-sun.com
Enzymes 2000, Elixir of Life, Intestinal Balance, Lipo-Metabolizer, Super Greens, Osteo Formula, Green Tea Formula, and Super Antioxidant	The Khader Group 39 Smith Avenue Mt. Kisco, NY 10549 (914) 242-0124 or 1-888-625-2008 Fax: (914) 242-5289 Web site: www.khadergroup.com E-mail: dkhader@khadergroup.com
Organic raw nuts, seeds, and dried fruit	Living Tree Community Foods P.O. Box 10082 Berkeley, CA 94709 1-800-260-5534 (510) 526-7106 Fax: (510) 526-9516 E-mail: organic97@aol.com
Bulk grains, flour, packaged grains/cereals, rice products, organic bulk, and organic groceries	Lundberg Family Farms 5370 Church Street Richvale, CA 95974 (530) 883-4551 Fax: (530) 882-4500 E-mail: timo@lundberg.com

Products	Manufacturer
Organic grocery	Made in Nature, Inc. 100 Stony Point Road, Suite 200 Santa Rosa, CA 95401-4133 (707) 535-400 Fax: (415) 535-4039
Bulk pastas, rice products, and wheat/yeast free products	Mrs. Leeper's 12455 Kerran Street, Suite 200 Poway, CA 92064 (619) 486-1101 Fax: (619) 486-1770 E-mail: mlpinc@pacbell.net
Refrigerated/frozen soy products, vinegars/salad dressings, condiments, spices, seasonings, and kosher/parve products	Nasoya Foods, Inc. One New England Way Ayer, MA 01432 (978) 772-6880 Fax: (978) 772-6881 E-mail: bdecosts@nasoya.com
Packaged grains/cereals, bulk cereals cookies, condiments, spices, seasonings, crackers, and organic groceries	New Morning, Inc. 25 Stow Road Boxboro, MA 01719-4773 (561) 641-5685 Fax: (561) 641-6509
Stevia sweeteners, full-line grocery	Now Foods 395 South Glen Ellyn Road Bloomingdale, IL 60108-2176 (630) 545-9098 Fax: (630) 545-9075 E-mail: sales@nowfoods.com

Products	Manufacturer
Organic dairy and bulk products, organic poultry, meats, and eggs	Organic Valley 507 W. Main Street La Farge, WI 54639 (608) 625-2602 Fax: (608) 625-2908 E-mail: pacgreen@teleport.com
Allergy-free grocery products, wheat/yeast-free products, cookies, packaged baking mixes, kosher/parve products, and specialty/gourmet products	Pamela's Products, Inc. 364 Littlefield Avenue South San Francisco, CA 94080-6103 (650) 952-4546 Fax: (650) 742-6643 E-mail: info@pamelasproducts.com
Organic, allergy-free, and kosher/parve products; and wheat/yeast-free products	Quinoa Corporation P.O. Box 1039 Torrance, CA 90505-1039 (310) 530-8666 Fax: (310) 530-8764 E-mail: quinoacorp@aol.com
Organic grocery, organic chocolates	Rapunzel Pure Organic Food 122 Smith Road P.O. Box 350 Dinderhood, NY 12106 1-800-207-2814 Fax: (518) 758-6439 E-mail: info@rapunzel.com
All types of spelt breads	Rudi's Bakery 3640 Walnut St., Unit B Boulder, CO 80301-2500 (303) 447-0495 Fax: (303) 447-0516 E-mail: sromer@rudisbakery.com

Products	Manufacturer
Tamari wheat-free organic soy sauce	San-J International, Inc. 2880 Sprouse Drive Richmond, VA 23231 1-800-446-5500 (804) 226-8333 Fax: (804) 226-8383 E-mail: sanj@richmond.infi.net
Organic nonfat yogurt	Stonyfield Farm Yogurt 10 Burton Drive Londonderry, NH 03053 (603) 437-4040 Fax: (603) 437-3935 www.stonyfield.com
Prepared Asian foods, such as kim chee	Sunja's Oriental Foods, Inc. 40 Foundry Street Waterbury, VT 05676-1503 (802) 244-7644 Fax: (802) 244-6880 E-mail: sunjas@madriver.com
Westbrae natural, stone-ground mustard; organic grocery; and soy products	Westbrae Natural Foods 1056 E. Walnut Street Carson, CA 90746 1-800-769-6455 Fax: (310) 886-8219
Organic produce, dried fruits, nuts, and seeds	Woodstock Organics, Inc. 126 Main Street New City, NY 10956 (914) 634-1419 Fax: (914) 634-1396 E-mail: woodstockorganics@worldnet.att.net

Endnotes

1   Doris Grant and Jean Joyce, *Food Combining for Health* (Rochester, Vt.: Healing Arts Press, 1989), 47.

2   Steve Meyerowitz, *Food Combining and Digestion* (Great Barrington, Mass.: The Sprout House, Inc., 1996), 51.

3   Thomas Kruzel, "Serotyping and Diet—Dietary Serotype Panel," *Townsend Letter for Doctors and Patients* (November 1996): 75.

4   W. A. Franklin, "Tissue Binding of Lectins in Disorders of the Breast," *Cancer* 51 (1983): 295–300.

5   David L. J. Freed, "Lectins in Food: Their Importance in Health and Disease," *Journal of Nutrition and Medicine* 2, no. 1 (1991): 45–65.

6   Peter D'Adamo with Catherine Whitney, *Eat Right for Your Type* (New York: G.P. Putnam's Sons, 1996), 54.

7   J. N. Livingston and B. J. Purvis, "Effects of Wheatgerm Agglutinin on Insulin Binding and Insulin Sensitivity of Fat Cells," *American Journal of Physiology* 238 (1980): E267–E75.

8   Humbart Santillo, *Food Enzymes: The Missing Link to Radiant Health* (Prescott, Ariz.: Hohm Press, 1987), 25.

9   Anthony J. Cichoke, *Enzymes and Enzyme Therapy* (Los Angeles: Keats Publishing, 1994), 38–39.

10   D. A. Lopez, R. M. Williams, and K. Miehlke, *Enzymes: The Fountain of Life* (Salem, Mass.: Neville Press, 1994), 112–16.

11   Barry Sears with Bill Lawren, *Enter the Zone* (New York: Harper Collins, 1995), 269–72.

12   Ann Louise Gittleman, *How to Stay Young and Healthy in a Toxic World* (Los Angeles: Keats Publishing, 1999), 21.

13   Barry Sears with Bill Lawren, *Enter the Zone*, 36.

14 David Richard, *Stevia Rebaudiana, Nature's Sweet Secret* (Thibodaux, La.: Blue Heron Press, 1996), 7

15 Je Klaunig, "Chemopreventive Effects of Green Tea Components on Hepatic Carcinogenesis," *Preventitive Medicine* 21 (1992): 510–19.

16 G. Assmann and H. Shulte, "Modeling the Helsinki Heart Study by Means of Risk Equations Obtained from the Procam Study and the Framingham Heart Study," *Drug* 40 (1990): Suppl 1: 138.

17 D. T. Nash, S. D. Nash, and W. D. Grant, "Grapeseed Oil, a Natural Agent Which Raises Serum HDL Levels," *Journal of American College of Cardiology* (1993): 925–1116.

Bibliography

Bland, Jeffrey, and Sarah Bynum. *Genetic Nutritioneering, Chapter 5*. Los Angeles: Keats Publishing, 1999.

Constantine, Peter. *What's Your Type? How Blood Types Are the Keys to Unlocking Your Personality*. New York: Plume Publication, 1997.

Covelli, V., et al. "Spontaneous Lymphomas in Mice Genetically Selected for High or Low Phytohemagglutinin Responsiveness." *Journal of National Cancer Institute* 75 (1985): 1083–90.

D'Adamo, Peter, with Catherine Whitney. *Eat Right for Your Type*. New York: G.P. Putnam's Sons, 1996.

Derwahl M., J. Barth, and K-G Ravens. "Mononuclear Cell Response to Lectins: CAMP and Chemiluminescence." In J. Breborowicz and T. C. Bog-Hansen, eds. *Lectins: Biology, Biochemistry, Clinical*, vol. IV, (1985): 39–44.

Drenth, J., et al. "The Toxin-Agglutinin Fold." *Journal of Biological Chemistry* 255 (1980): 2653–55.

Fabian, R. H., and J. D. Coulter. "Transneuronal Transport of Lectins." *Brain Research* 344 (1985): 21–28.

Fischer, J., and B. Csillik. "Lectin Binding: A Genuine Marker for Trans-ganglinoic Regulation of Human Primary Sensory Neurons." *Neuroscience Letter* 54 (1985): 263–67.

Freed, David L.J. "Laboratory Diagnosis of Food Intolerance." In J. Brostoff and S. J. Challacombe, eds. *Food Allergy and Food Intolerance* (1987): 877–878.

—— "Lectins, Allergens, and Mucus." In T.C. Bog-Hansen, ed. *Lectins: Biology, Biochemistry, Clinical Biology* 2 (1982): 33–43.

Gibbons, R. J., and I. Dankers. "Lectin-like Constituents in Food, Which React with Components of Human Serum, Saliva, and Streptococcus Mutans." *Applied Environmental Microbiology* 41 (1981): 880–88.

Goo, Yu, et al. "Reduced Risk of Esophageal Cancer Associated with Green Tea Consumption." *Journal of National Cancer Institute* 86, no. 11 (June 1 1994): 855–58.

Grant, G. "Metabolic and Hormonal Responses to Dietary Lectins." In *Mini-symposium on Lectins*, 4-6 March 1986.

Hay, William Howard. *A New Health Era* (out of print). Copies available at secondhand bookstores.

Huz, Toda M., et al. "Mitogenic Activity of Epigallocatechin Gallate on ß-cells and Investigation of Its Structure Function Relationship." *International Journal of Immunopharmacology* 14, no. 8 (1992): 1399–1407.

Kruzel, Thomas A. "Serotyping and Diet: Dietary Serotype Panel." *Townsend Letter for Doctors and Patients* (November 1996).

Lipski, Elizabeth. *Digestive Wellness*. Los Angeles: Keats Publishing, 1996.

Mourant, A. E. *Blood Relations: Blood Groups and Anthropology*. Oxford, England: Oxford University Press, 1983.

Nachasbar, M., et al. "Lectins in the United States Diet: A Survey of Lectins in Commonly Consumed Foods and a Review of the Literature." *American Journal of Clinical Nutrition* 33 (1980).

Nomi, T., and A. Besher. *You Are Your Blood Type*. New York: Pocket Books, 1998.

Power, Laura. "Dietary Lectins, Food Allergy and Blood Type Specificity." *Townsend Letter for Doctors and Patients* (June 1991).

Shelton, Herbert M. *Food Combining Made Easy*. San Antonio, Tex.: Willow Publishing, 1985.

Taylor, Nadine. *Green Tea, the Natural Secret for a Healthier Life*. New York: Kensington Health, 1998.

Teisner, B., et al. "The Third Complement Factor (C3) and Its in Vivo Clevage Products: Interaction with Lectins and Precipitation with Polyethylene Glycol." *Journal of Immunological Methods* 66 (1984): 112–18.

Tolson, N. D., T. D. Daley, and G. P. Wysocki. "Lectin Probes of Glyconjugates in Human Salivary Glands." *Journal of Oral Pathology & Medicine* 14 (1985): 523–30.

Triadou, N., and E. Audran. "Interaction of Gamma-glutamyltransferase from Human Tissues with Insolubilized Lectins." *Clinical Biochemistry* 12 (1979): 256–60.

Yagisawa, H., et al. "Interactions of Brain Muscarinic Acetylcholine Receptors with Plant Lectins." *Journal of Biochemistry* (Tokyo) 98 (1985): 705–11.

Zahnley, J. C. "Stability of Enzyme Inhibitors and Lectins in Foods and the Influence of Specific Binding Interactions." *Advances in Experimental Medicine and Biology* 177 (1984): 333–65.

Zavazal, V., and V. Krauz. "Lectin Binding Ability of Immunoglobulin E and Its Participation in Triggering of Mast Cells." *Folia Biologica* (Prague) 30 (1985): 237–46.

A

A blood type

beans list, 36

best foods for, 5–6

beverages list, 39

dairy products list, 34–35

evolution of, 5–6

fish and shellfish list, 33–34

food combining chart, 40

fresh fruits and vegetables list, 38–39

grains for, 36–37

low-starch vegetables for, 37–38

maintenance menus, sample, 42–43

meats and eggs list, 33

nuts and seeds for, 35–36

oils list, 35

starchy vegetables list, 37

success story, 15–16

vegetarian diet and, 5–6, 15

weight-loss menus, sample, 41–42

wheat and, 10

AB blood type

beans list, 56

beverages list, 59–60

dairy products list, 55

evolution of, 6

exercise and, 8

fish and shellfish list, 54–55

food combining charts, 61

foods for, 6

fresh fruits and juices list, 59

grains for, 57

low-starch vegetables list, 58

maintenance menus, sample, 62–63

nuts and seeds list, 56

oils list, 56

starchy vegetables list, 57

success story, 17

weight-loss menus, sample, 60–61

wheat and, 17

acid environment, and protein foods, 1

acid enzymes, and alkaline enzymes, 1–2

Adele's Asian Adventure with Fish and Veggies, 100–101

aerobic exercise, 7

aging, and enzyme production, 9

Aioli Sauce, 104

alkaline enzymes

acid enzymes and, 1–2

starches and carbohydrates and, 1–2

allergies, food

anaphylactic shock and, 3

lectins and, 4

neutralized environment and, 2–3

anaphylactic shock, and food allergies, 3

antioxidants, in green tea, 13

B

E

eating speed, 3

eggs. *See also* meats and eggs list

    Almond Meringues, 124

    Dilled Egg or Tuna Salad, Delectable, 68

    Just Custard, 120

environment, peaceful, 3–4

enzyme deficiencies, diseases linked to, 9

enzyme supplements, benefits of, 9–10

enzymes

    aging and, 9

    animal-based, 10

    for weight loss, 8–10

    plant, 9, 10

Enzymes 2000, 26

Escarole, Garlic, 87

evolution of blood types, 5–6

F

family meals, recipes compatible with all blood types for, 64–66

fasting, 13–14

    recommended methods, 13–14

    sample one-day juice fast, 14

fat cells in body, 8

Fennel Broccoli Slaw, 87

Fennel, Roasted, 88

Fennel, Sautéed, with Seared Tuna, 106

fish and shellfish

    Adele's Asian Adventure with Fish and Veggies, 100–101

    Baked Tandoori Fish, 105

    Basic Broiled Fish, 101–102

    Basic Poached Fish, 103–104

    Broiled Fish Kabobs, 103

    Broiled Fish with a Zip, 102

    Codfish Salad, 71–72

    Dilled Egg or Tuna Salad, Delectable, 68

    Giovanna's Sautéed Tuna, 105–106

    Seared Tuna with Sautéed Fennel, 106

fish and shellfish list

    for A blood type, 33–34

    for AB blood type, 54–55

    for B blood type, 43–44

    for O blood type, 22–23

flaxseed oil, 16

food allergies. *See* allergies, food

food combining

    concept of, 1–2

    food allergies in relation to, 2–3

    symptoms produced by, 2

food combining charts

    A blood type, 40

    AB blood type, 61

    B blood type, 51

    O blood type, 29

    arrangement of, 19

I

immune system
  food allergies and, 2–3
  sugar and, 11
Indian-Spiced Spinach Soup, 80–81
inflammation, and incompatible
    lectins, 4
insulin/insulin levels
  cancer and, 12
  corn and, 10
  gluten and, 5
  sugar and, 11–12
  wheat and, 10

J

juices. *See also* fruits and juices, fresh,
    list
  Cranberry Delight, 14
  Ginger Jazz, 14
  Metabolic Booster, 14
  Pineapple Pizzazz, 14
Just Custard, 120

K

Kabobs, Broiled Fish, 103
Kasha (Buckwheat) Pilaf, 99

L

Lactobacillus acidophilus, 15–16
Lactobacillus bifidus, 15

lamb
  Broiled Boneless Butterflied Leg of
      Lamb, 115
  Herb-Crusted Roast Leg of Lamb,
      114
lectins, 4–5
  cancer and, 4, 5
  defined, 4
  harmful, 4–5
Leeks, Spiced, 88
Lemon-Garlic-Oregano Dressing, 74
Lentil Soup, Creamy, 78
Lentils with Spinach, 92
leukemia, 5
lipase, 8
Low-Cal Yogurt Dressing, 75

M

magnesium citrate, 26
maintenance of weight. *See* weight-
    maintenance menus, sample
Marinated Broiled Chicken, 111
Marinated Cold Asparagus, 83
Mayonnaise, Basic, 73
Mayonnaise, Curry, 74
meats and eggs list
  for A blood type, 33
  for AB blood type, 54
  for B blood type, 43
  for O blood type, 22
Mediterranean Vegetable Soup, 81

Breast, 107–108

Grilled Turkey Tenderloins, 108–109

Turkey Moussaka, 109–110

Turkey or Chicken Cutlets with Lemon, 107

U

ulcers, and plant enzymes, 9

Ultra-Clear Plus, 14

Ultra-GlycemX, 14

V

Vegetable Chicken Soup, Grandma's, 79–80

Vegetable Soup, Mediterranean, 81

vegetables. *See also* soups

Adele's Asian Adventure with Fish and Veggies, 100–101

Baked Zucchini, 90

Bean Dip and Crudités, 95

Broccoli or String Beans Oriental, 84–85

Broccoli Rabe, Italian Style, 85

Cauliflower with Indian Spices, 85–86

Cold Oriental Bean Sprouts, 84

Cucumber and Yogurt Raita, 86

Fennel Broccoli Slaw, 87

Garlic Escarole, 87

Marinated Cold Asparagus, 83

Roasted Fennel, 88

Slightly Sautéed Spinach with Garlic, 89

Spiced Leeks, 88

Spinach with Yogurt, 90

Steamed Greens, 91

String Beans with Shallots or Lemon, 89

Zucchini with Fresh Herbs, 91

vegetables, low-starch, list

for A blood type, 37–38

for AB blood type, 58

for B blood type, 47–48

for O blood type, 26–27

vegetables, starchy, list

for A blood type, 37

for AB blood type, 57

for B blood type, 47

for O blood type, 26

vegetarian diet

A blood type and, 5–6

O blood type and, 5

Vinaigrette, Curry, 76

Vinaigrette, Mustard, 76

vitamin E, 15

W

water retention, and weight loss, 2–3

weight gain

eating quickly and, 3

O blood type and, 5

water retention and, 2–3

weight loss

A blood type and, 6

B blood type and, 6

detoxifying products and, 14

elimination of allergenic foods
and, 2–4

enzymes for, 8–10

exercise and, 7–8

focus on, 7

optimal, suggestion for, 20

success stories, 15–18

weight-loss and weight-maintenance
meals, 19–66

A blood type sample menus, 41–43

AB blood type sample menus,
60–63

B blood type sample menus,
50, 52–53

O blood type sample menus,
30–32

weight-loss menus, sample

for A blood type, 41–42

for AB blood type, 60–61

for B blood type, 50, 52

for O blood type, 30–31

weight-maintenance menus, sample,
19–20

for A blood type, 42–43

for AB blood type, 62–63

for B blood type, 52–53

for O blood type, 30–31, 31–32

weight training, 8

wheat

AB blood type and, 6, 17

B blood type and, 6

bleached, 10–11

elimination of, 10

harmfulness of, 10–11

O blood type and, 5, 16

products containing, 11

wild yam root, 15

Y

yoga, 8

yogurt

Cold Yogurt and Cucumber Soup,
77–78

Cucumber and Yogurt Raita, 86

Low-Cal Yogurt Dressing, 75

Yummy Brownies, 125

Z

Zucchini with Fresh Herbs, 91

Zucchini, Baked, 90